LEADERSHIP LESSONS FROM THE
Medicine Wheel

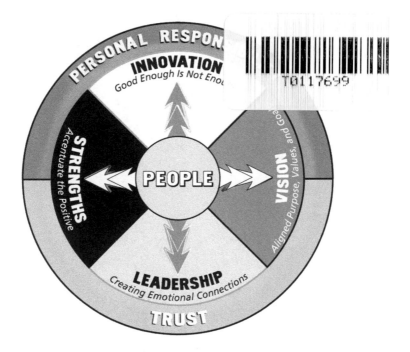

www.LeadershipLessonsFromTheMedicineWheel.com

LEADERSHIP LESSONS FROM THE
Medicine Wheel

The Seven Elements of
High Performance

Gary Lear

Published by Advantage, Charleston, South Carolina.
Member of Advantage Media Group.

ADVANTAGE is a registered trademark and the Advantage colophon is a trademark of Advantage Media Group, Inc.

Printed in the United States of America.

ISBN: 978-1-59932-111-0
LCCN: 2009907353

This publication is designed to provide accurate and authoritative information in regard to the subject matter covered. It is sold with the understanding that the publisher is not engaged in rendering legal, accounting, or other professional services. If legal advice or other expert assistance is required, the services of a competent professional person should be sought.

Most Advantage Media Group titles are available at special quantity discounts for bulk purchases for sales promotions, premiums, fundraising, and educational use. Special versions or book excerpts can also be created to fit specific needs.

For more information, please write: Special Markets, Advantage Media Group, P.O. Box 272, Charleston, SC 29402 or call 1.866.775.1696.

Visit us online at **advantagefamily**.com

Dedication

For my family and friends.

Special thanks to my best friends, John Bentley and Mike Boozer, for allowing me to bounce ideas around with them and for the many great discussions that we have had throughout the years.

I would like to thank my early mentors for helping me on the two life paths that converged:

Rick Knight

Keith Ayers

Rob Lebow

Randy Spitzer

For my wife Ann.

She put up with years of listening to me talk about research and my ideas that came from that research. She provided invaluable feedback and support. I couldn't have done it without her.

Table of Contents

Introduction

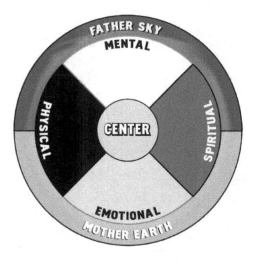

The Seven Elements of High Performance model is not something that I created, but rather something that I have discovered. It is the result of the convergence of two separate journeys that I began many years ago.

One journey began at the end of 2001. I had just completed a one-year project at Educational Testing Service where I had been engaged to create a new division. As a result, I had spent a considerable amount of time working away from my home and family. Now that the project was over I was again marketing my training and consulting services to a variety of potential clients. Yet, I found myself rather unmotivated to go back to doing one-day and two-day training programs that, in the end, had little or no real impact on the operations of my clients' organizations. I was chomping at the bit to apply some of my education and experience to make a real long-term difference for my clients' and their organizations.

But what actually did make a real difference? That was a huge question, as there were literally hundreds of theories and approaches out there in research articles and in management books. The last thing I wanted to do was to be told that I was bringing yet another "fad" to a client. There must be a handful of simple things that any organization could do that would have a real and lasting impact on performance. All I needed to do was find them.

I began reading all manner of research studies, articles, and books about research, focusing specifically on high-performance organizations and larger scale, long-term research. It was all too easy to point out how they all differed. In fact, I had come across several articles that had done just that, stating that obviously if none could agree then there was no value to any of them. Yet, I believed that there was value, and I was finding areas where there was agreement. I began to focus my efforts on finding not what they were saying that was different, but rather on finding what they were all saying that was the same.

I began to see patterns develop, and several themes began to emerge. First it was just a few, and then I began to see more, some of these coalescing into a single, more robust theme. Finally, there were seven very robust themes, or elements of high performance, that had emerged from the hundreds of research articles and almost three years of study.

As these seven elements emerged, I not only noticed an interrelationship between each element and the other elements, I also noticed that there was a very strong relationship of these seven elements to something else entirely, leading to what I had thought was a totally unrelated previous and personal journey.

In 1991 I had made a decision to learn more about my American Indian heritage; a heritage that my family had spent generations hiding.

After all, it wasn't desirable to be Cherokee in the mid-1800s to mid-1900s. But some personal things had happened in my life that led to a desire to learn more about the history, culture and beliefs of Cherokees, my matrilineal heritage, as well as other native peoples in North and South America.

I devoured a variety of books about my heritage, and attended a great number of powwows and other cultural events where I met a variety of people. There was the Apache elder who taught me about hair and its connection to spirituality; the Pueblo teacher who taught me about justice; and many others, each with their own special lesson. One of the events that had the most impact was when I stopped at a little store in North Florida where I met a Miccosukee elder who taught classes on the Medicine Wheel each week, which I soon began attending. Slowly but steadily my journey of learning continued, and it still continues today, as I am always trying to learn more about my heritage and how I can apply that learning to my life.

The Medicine Wheel became a simple yet very complex and powerful structure for relating a lot of other concepts that I was dealing with, both personally and professionally. I had already begun to see some connections with some American Indian philosophies to best business practices. And then, as the themes began to emerge in my research I saw the connection between the Medicine Wheel and these themes.

The two journeys had converged.

What I am about to share with you is the story of this convergence and my discovery. Yes, the Seven Elements of High Performance™ is exactly that: a discovery. It is not something that I have crafted to "fit" a preconceived model that I set out to develop, but rather, it is a naturally occurring model that works precisely because it was discovered and not contrived. The research says that these seven things work together to bring about high performance; the Medicine Wheel tells us why these seven things work.

And with that, let's begin at the beginning...

The Medicine Wheel

For all the people of the earth, the Creator has planted a Sacred Tree under which we may gather, and there will find healing, power, wisdom, and security.

The roots of this tree spread deep into body of our Mother Earth. Its branches reach upwards like hands praying to Father Sky.

The fruits of this tree are the good things Creator has given to his people: Teachings that show the path to Love, Wisdom, Justice, Patience, Compassion, Generosity, Courage, and those which bring balance into our lives: Honor, Dignity, and Respect.

THE SACRED TREE

These are the beginning words of the workbook, *The Sacred Tree*, which was given to me when I first began to learn about the Medicine Wheel. It was the result of a group of elders from a great many American Indian Nations coming together at a conference to share about the teachings of the Medicine Wheel. As with many people who had not grown up learning about the Medicine Wheel, I had an idea of what it was, but did not fully appreciate the depth and richness that was waiting there for me to discover.

Many think that the Medicine Wheel is a physical thing that has special power. They may point to a set of rocks that have been put in a ritualistic pattern, or perhaps a smaller item that is in the form of a circle with certain colors. While these things might be called Medicine

Wheels, they are not *The* Medicine Wheel. They are only physical manifestations, or symbols, of The Medicine Wheel. The Medicine Wheel is simply a concept.

The Medicine Wheel is a concept that helps us better understand other concepts that are not physical in nature and, thus, not always easily understood. As the Sacred Tree says, "Just like a mirror can be used to see things not normally visible (behind us or around a corner), the Medicine Wheel can be used to help us see or understand things we can't quite see or understand because they are ideas and not physical objects."

While the colors of the locations and the specific meanings of the locations might vary slightly from American Indian nation to nation, the concept of the Medicine Wheel is fairly consistent across North and South America. For example, one nation might put the color Red in the East, while another nation might put it in the South. One nation might use the color Black, while another nation might use the color Blue, or Brown or even Green. Yet while these colors and their locations might differ, the basic concepts remain fairly similar.

What I am about to share with you is the location, colors, and meanings that I learned through my study of the Medicine Wheel in the book *The Sacred Tree*, as well as from other sources. If you have learned something different then I am sure you will find strong similarities between what I share and the Medicine Wheel you learned.

The Directions of the Medicine Wheel

The Medicine Wheel is the concept of a circle and Seven Sacred Directions. The Four Cardinal Directions, along with Center, are what are the most common when people refer to the Medicine Wheel. These directions, colors, and corresponding concepts are as follows:

East: This is the direction of the dawn and of new beginnings, and is often symbolized by the color Red. This is the direction of the **Spiritual** aspect. It is a location or time where we place emphasis on *determining*, and such things as hope, potential, and insights for the future. It is also a time of spontaneity.

South: This is the direction of the mid-day and of youth, and is often symbolized by the color Yellow. This is the direction of the **Emotional** aspect. It is a location or time where we place emphasis on *relationships*, and such things as sacrifice, compassion and loyalty. It is also a time of transformation.

West: This is the direction of the setting sun and of maturity, and is often symbolized by the color of Black. It is the direction of the **Physical** aspect. It is a location or time where we place emphasis on *holding* what we have, and such things as perseverance and development of our unique gifts. It is also a time of introspection and self-knowledge.

North: This is the direction of night and of rebirth and renewal, and is often symbolized by the color White. It is the direction of the **Mental** aspect. It is a location or time where we place emphasis on *receiving*, and such things as solving problems, creating abundance, and completing things. It is also a time for application of knowledge.

Center: This is the balance point. It is the direction of Self, and more collectively, *The People*. This is the *soul*, where we find integration and wholeness. It is also where we find the spark that ignites the other four aspects. It is the location for our will and self-determination.

In some ways we can consider that these five directions are within us and define aspects of ourselves or times in our lives. There are also two additional Sacred Directions which are outside of us, yet still related and connected to us. They very much impact us and how we live our lives. They provide the foundations and context for our lives.

Down: This is the direction of Mother Earth, who is our foundation and from which all life flows. Without Mother Earth we cease to exist. Mother Earth provides us with the simple things that we need to build what we want out of our lives. While tough and resilient, we can easily destroy the gifts she provides us with thoughtless carelessness.

Up: This is the direction of Father Sky, our foundation above us. This direction is also referred to as the Sky Vault. It speaks to us of what we can achieve in our lives and provides us with encouragement to make the decisions that we need to make. (Please Note: Father Sky is not the same as Creator or God.)

The Circle

The richness of the Medicine Wheel begins to emerge as we look at how the Seven Sacred Directions begin to relate to each other as we examine things that are happening in our own lives. Out of this relationship we begin to see some additional concepts emerge. The first is that of the Circle. Everything exists within this Circle, and the perspective you see is based on where you stand in the Circle. Therefore, we begin to learn that it is not about being right or wrong, but about being effective in what we are trying to achieve in our lives that becomes the important focus.

Because everything does exist within the Circle, the concept of the Circle also teaches us that everything is related. There is interconnectedness to all things, as nothing exists on its own. We begin to understand that individual things only have real importance within their context of the overall whole. So while we might examine a thing in great detail, it must also be examined in regard to its surroundings and generalities, as well.

Also as opposed to straight lines and continuums, what we begin to see are relationships that have no beginnings and no ends, but are circular. We begin to move away from thoughts of "this *or* that" to those that are more inclusive, such as "this *and* that." We begin to understand that opposites are not at the extreme ends of a line, but connected to each other by the circumference of the Circle. Where one opposite ends the other begins, often with a blurring between the two where they meet.

The concept of a Circle also reminds us that there is no real beginning and no real end, yet things are always moving and in a state of change. American Indian philosophy has always believed that life is in constant change. Yet, with change there is always stability that comes from the cycles that are a part of nature. Our foundational beliefs also provide us with stability from the many changes we face across our lifetimes.

Balance

Another concept that emerges is that of Balance. Balance is not the same as being equal. When two things are equal it means that they are the same. When we talk about Balance we learn that sometimes we have to address issues not in an equal fashion, but in a manner to offset other forces that might be in play. If you think of a plate that is balanced perfectly on your finger, the balance point might be in the center of the plate. If you put an item on top of the plate to one side, then the balance point changes. It has to shift towards the opposite edge of the plate from where the object is in order to keep the plate balanced on the tip of the finger.

The same thing is true when we deal with issues in our lives, whether in our personal lives or at work. While we strive to achieve Balance, sometimes we have to put more effort or resources in an area that is in need of attention because of other forces that are in play. The trick is to not allow other areas of our lives to suffer in order to regain our balance. If this occurs then rather than progressing in our lives through continuous growth, we become stagnant, or worse, deteriorate.

As we address people and things in our lives, Balance teaches us that in order to be fair that we should not treat people or things equally, but in a way that is necessary to bring about harmony and to achieve our goals. I believe that this is a key concept regarding Balance, as too often we try to be fair by treating everyone equally, and in the end we just end up making a situation worse.

Self-Determination

One last concept that I would like to mention is that of Self-Determination and Non-Interference. One of the most central tenants of American Indian philosophy is that no one has the right to interfere with the lives of someone else. Everyone has the right to make their own choices, and, in fact, is obligated to make their own choices. Volition, or will, is, in essence, inherent in the Center of the Medicine Wheel, and therefore, in all of us. No one should force another to do something, and no one should allow another to force them to do something.

However, while we have the right to make our own decisions, we have the obligation to not make those decisions based solely on our own desires. We must keep in mind our obligations to others, including our family, friends, community, and, yes, even those at work. Coupled with the right of the Freedom of Choice comes the obligation of Responsibility of Commitment to self and others.

The Making of a Book

The Seven Sacred Directions of the Medicine Wheel and the concepts and lessons that emerge from them are the very foundation for success in any organization, and from them we see and can understand the Seven Elements of High Performance. I must admit that at first I was happy that I had begun to have a better understanding of the model and was fairly satisfied with that. In the mean time I had put a crude rendition of the model up on my website and had placed a rudimentary white paper on the subject with it, and thought nothing more about it.

Then one day I received contact from the US Navy. They told me that they were in the process of revising some of their leadership programs at the Center for Naval Leadership, and that they liked my model and wanted permission to use it in several of the programs. Of course, I said yes. I then offered to talk about the model at a couple of professional organizations, including the Organizational Development Network in Jacksonville, Florida. I was overwhelmed with the reaction that I received from them as they were so excited about how the model worked and how powerful it was. Several people said that I must write a book about it and that they wanted copies. Over the course of the next year I received similar reactions, and so I decided to finally try to put down in words just how the model of the Seven Elements of High Performance works.

In the pages that follow I will share with you a little about the research and try to give you an understanding of each of the Seven Elements. While I will share some of the research in this book, please keep in mind that this is not a book purely about research, but about lessons from the Medicine Wheel as they relate to the research.

I hope you enjoy.

The Attributes of the Medicine Wheel

NORTH
Receives

Teacher – Buffalo

Time – Future

Mental

Social/Political

Abundance

Completion

Solving Problems

Application of Knowledge

Innovation

WEST	CENTER	EAST
Holding	Soul	Determining
Teachers – Bear & Turtle		Teachers – Mouse & Eagle
Time – Present		Time – Momentary
Physical	Self	Spiritual
Economic	Volition/Will	Culture
Perseverance	Dwelling/Home	Spontaneity
Development of Gifts	Spark	Hope
Unique Purpose	Integration	Beginnings
	Wholeness	Potential
Introspections/Self Knowledge	Balance	Insights
Innovation	*People*	*Vision*

SOUTH
Giving

Teacher – Wolf

Time – Past

Emotional

Relationships

Sacrifice

Compassion

Loyalty

Transformations

Leadership

The Seven Elements of High Performance™

- Put **People** at the *Center* of everything you do; employees, customers, and community

- Build **Trust** as a *Foundation*

- Allow **Personal Responsibility** through *Individual Decision Making*

- Share a **Vision** of an *Aligned Purpose, Values, and Goals*

- *Create Emotional Connections* through **Leadership**

- Focus on **Strengths** and *Accentuate the Positive*

- Encourage **Innovation**, because *Good Enough is Not Enough*

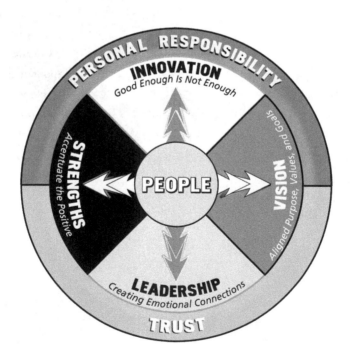

CHAPTER 1

The Case for High Performance

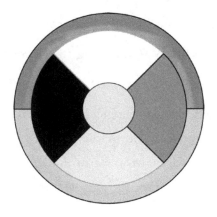

One of the things that fascinated me as I delved into the research about what drives high performance was the significant impact that the Seven Elements of High Performance have on the performance of an organization. Research study after research study trumpeted the significant difference between those organizations that were high performing and their next nearest competitor. Time after time and study after study I was seeing an average difference of anywhere from 700% up to over 1500% better performance. Keep in mind that the comparative organizations that the high performance organizations were being evaluated against weren't just average organizations in their industries; they weren't just good organizations in their industries; they were the high performance organization's nearest competitor!

One of the largest bodies of research is the ongoing studies by the Gallup Organization. Their research includes over a million people, thousands of managers, and hundreds of organizations. It also looks at performance in specific work units over a couple of decades. Their findings on the difference in performance is but one example:

The most "engaged" workplaces (top 25%) were:

- **50% more likely to have lower *staff turnover***
- **56% more likely to have high *customer loyalty***
- **38% more likely to have high *productivity***
- **27% more likely to report higher *profitability***

These are clearly significant differences in performance. So why would any organization want to settle for being just "average" or for being "good enough?" I believe that the reason for settling for less than high performance comes from three primary factors.

The first factor is that most organizations haven't identified what performance means to them. While all of the studies that I reviewed took the time to identify what performance meant in the context of their study, most organizations fail to define what performance means for them. Instead, they allow others to identify what performance means, and most of the time it is in the realm of finances, typically revenue, profits, or stock price.

This is limiting for a number of reasons, but primarily because most financial measures are lagging indicators of future performance. By the time we are able to obtain our financial measures the time to take action to impact them has already passed. All we can do from that point is to take actions to impact our future financial measures, and by the time we have those measures, once again, the time to take action has already passed. Any way you look at it, financial measures only tell you how well you have done, not how well you will do, or what you must do to be successful.

Secondly, some of these financial measures just don't really apply to the majority of organizations in America. While larger organizations might have to worry about stock prices and need to have elaborate accounting procedures (although that position might be debatable), most organizations in America are not publicly traded. They are small businesses, which account for about half of all employees in America today. While finances are certainly important, they are not the driving force for success that seems to be the focus for those publically traded organizations.

So if finances aren't the best way to define performance, then what is? Well, that depends on the organization. As a matter of fact, the definition of performance is what ever a given organization decides it wants it to be. But all too often organizations haven't taken the time to figure that out. They don't know what is really important to them and their organization's success or how they will define performance and how they will measure it.

This leads us to the second factor for why most organizations are satisfied with being "good enough," which is *Intent*. This is a very important concept, both from a research point of view, as well as how it relates to the Medicine Wheel. Intent in this case does not mean just wishing to do something, as it is often used. You might often hear someone say "I intended to lose some weight but just never got around to it," or "I intended to exercise more, but my life is just too busy to find time." This is not an example of *Intent*, but an example of just wishing with no intent at all to accomplish what the person has said they want to accomplish.

Intent is about making a conscious decision to accomplish something and then setting out to take action to accomplish it. It is about being aware of one's self, one's surroundings, and the energy that will be needed to accomplish the desired outcome and committing to making it happen. The Medicine Wheel speaks about all of us having Volition, or Will; the ability to make our own decisions and take action based on those decisions. *Intent* also involves a sense of urgency about what you are setting out to do. Intent isn't about getting around to things when we might have time to do them, which so often never occurs. *Intent* is about making those things important and finding the time to do them. In the research, as well as my experience in studying and working with High Performance Organizations, all of them made a conscious decision to be great at what they were doing. They *intended* to be the best, and set out to do things that would bring this about, making those things important.

On the other hand, those organizations that weren't high performing had no such *Intent*. All they wanted to do was either make money or just survive. Their focus was usually on other areas and not on identifying what performance meant and what they needed to do to make performance happen on a consistent basis. All too often these organizations make weak plans for action, and are often changing those plans due to a variety of circumstances impacting negatively on the organization. Instead of being proactive, these organizations are always being reactive, consuming huge amounts of resources to just keep up. After all, how often have you seen organizations create a five-year "strategic" plan, then revise it every year as if it is only a one-year strategic plan, and then don't use it until it is time to once again revise it?

The difference is that the leadership of high performance organizations takes the time to work *on* their organizations, not just work *in* their organizations. They realize that it is just as important to take the time to know what is important to the long-term success of the organization and to figure out how to measure it, as it is to be doing day-to-day activities. They realize that without taking the time to know what is important that they just can't effectively prioritize the day-to-day activities so that they do what really needs to be done to impact performance for the long-term.

The leadership of average organizations, on the other hand, rarely takes the time to figure out what is really important. Often this results in constantly moving from one crisis to the next, and a mentality of thinking that everything is important. They believe that they just don't have the time to sit down and do that "strategic planning stuff," and that it wouldn't do much good, anyway because "things change too often." Instead of taking control of their organization, they allow control to be given up to their external surroundings.

I can't stress enough the importance of this concept of *Intent* on the success of implementing the Seven Elements in any organization. If you are not willing to devote the time, energy, and resources to put the Seven Elements to work for you then you will not become a high performance organization. It is that simple. If you believe that you are already "good enough" then you will not become a high performance organization, and most likely you will actually fall behind.

It is all too easy to fool yourself into believing that you really do intend to be a high performance organization. For example, I once had a client, a small organization of about 300 employees, which fell into this trap. I was doing some work with their top leadership, and I shared with them that I was only willing to work with those organizations that desired to be the best. I received a rather harsh reaction from several of the leaders, many who stated, "Why would anyone want to be anything else?" Why indeed! In the end, when it came time for them to actually have to change their behavior and management approaches, they balked and resisted because they had "always done things this way" and that things were "good enough." In the end I cancelled the project because I was wasting my time and they were wasting their money. Nothing was going to change because there was a lack of **Intent** to do what it would take achieve higher levels of performance for the organization.

The third factor that leads to so few organizations achieving high levels of performance is that most organizations focus on performance at the wrong level. If you want to achieve high levels of organizational performance then it is all about organizational performance. Period! Let me say that again; if you want high levels of organizational performance, then you must, I repeat, must focus on organizational performance, not individual performance. While individuals do contribute to the success of organizational performance, focusing on increasing individual performance will most likely not lead to organizational performance.

As a young boy, I remember hearing about a particular famous football player. He was a running back for a pro team in the northeast. As I recall, it seems that weekend after weekend there were reports about this particular player rushing for a tremendous amount of yardage, sometimes breaking records. At the end of almost every story they concluded that despite the great performance of this football star, the team lost yet another game.

Contrast this to a baseball team from several years ago. At the time they were a team of relatively unknown baseball players, all working very hard at their respective jobs. While no one was remarkable or thought of as "a star," the team had a highly successful year and went on to play in the World Series and won.

What these two stories tell us is that it doesn't take extraordinary performance by any one individual to give us high performance. Instead, what is needed is good solid performance by everyone working together and focused on a few key things that drive performance for the organization. Yet, what most organizations do is create highly complicated systems where they attempt to measure and manage individual performance. Unfortunately, most of these systems aren't designed to focus that individual performance back to organizational performance.

In fact, most people don't know what they need to do in order to impact the goals of their organization. In a Harris poll a few years ago they discovered that 51% of employees do not understand what they personally need to do to help the organization achieve its goals. Employees also reported that they only spend about 49% of their time working on things that might impact those goals. What is worse is that only 15% of employees could even identify their organization's top goals. This is usually because organizations don't have clearly defined goals, or if they do have goals then they aren't being clearly communicated. How, then, does the ability to make an employee a higher level performer help the organization perform better if the employee's increased performance isn't focused on the organization's performance? If we want to have a high performance organization then we must focus on the things that make the organization perform, beginning with how we define and measure performance and then how we cascade that down through the organization.

These three factors, defining performance, intending to be high performing, and focusing on organizational performance, are the three keys to unlocking the potential of the Seven Elements of High Performance. Actually, two of the three keys, defining performance and focusing on organizational performance, are accomplished by working with the Seven Elements. It is *Intent* that is essential in order to get started.

The Will: The doorway through which all must pass if they wish to become more than they are now is the doorway of the will. A person must decide to take the journey. It will always be there for those who decide to travel through it.

THE SACRED TREE

I want to share one final thought with you before we begin discussing the Seven Elements of High Performance that is vital to making the model work for your organization. Simply put, the best organizations don't do the same things that the rest of the organizations do. This simple concept was shared first in the book *First Break All the Rules* by Gallup, and later on in a variety of other books such as *Built to Last* and *Good to Great,* all books based on long-term research. The concept was further supported by a variety of other research studies that I reviewed. Simply put, most organizations function at a level surrounding the average, and while good, they aren't the best. As we've seen, the research shows us that the best don't just out perform the average by a little bit; they out perform the average by a lot.

So if you want to be better than the average, if you want to be better than "good enough," then you will have to do things that are different than what everyone else is doing, and probably a bit different than you've done things in the past in your organization. The Seven Elements of High Performance are the things that can provide you with the different things to be doing that will make that difference for you in your organization. So let's learn more about these Seven Elements.

The Central Element

CHAPTER 2

Put People at the *Center* of Everything You Do;

Employees, Customers, and Community

There is danger for any traveler, should they attempt to dwell forever in any of the directions. For the place of dwelling is in the center of the universe, and it is to the center that we must always return, for it is our true home.

THE SACRED TREE

T he Medicine Wheel teaches us that we have to place ourselves in the center in order to find balance. In the center is where we will find our Will, or Volition, or as I have called it in the previous chapter, *Intent*. It is where we will also find our balance for our own Will in relation to others. In other words, it is where we balance our concern for ourselves against the concern we have for others; it is where we find the integration of the individual into the whole of the pPeople. It is a duality of retaining an individual's integrity as it also belongs to and serves the whole.

In American Indian beliefs, no one can tell another person what they should do. Each person is an individual and is free to choose their own path and to make their own decisions. Yet, there is also the concept of sacrifice for the good of others, where individuals will not be told what to do, but will chose on their own to do the things that will be best for all. Everything that is done is done for the good of the People.

During the beginning of my research I was affiliated with a small group of independent consultants. We were working to try to put together a more comprehensive approach to helping organizations perform. I was initially attracted to the group because it was focused on the same things as I was focused on, and, in fact, being affiliated with it helped me gain some focus in my early days of research.

As part of our early research we used to go around talking to groups of executives and managers about some of our ideas in executive briefings. We would begin our briefings by asking the attending executives and managers a few simple questions:

- What challenges are you and your organization facing over the next five to ten years?

- What are the business implications if you fail to successfully deal with these challenges?

- What kinds of people will you need to effectively deal with these challenges?

- Where will you find them and how will you retain them?

As we asked these questions we began to see an increasingly similar pattern regarding the kinds of people that these managers said that they needed to overcome their business challenges. These included:

• Willing to learn	• Team players
• Receptive to change	• Competent
• Committed	• Talented
• Creative	• Responsible
• Innovative	• Open-minded
• Self-starters	• Proactive
• Self-motivated	• Honest

These managers already knew instinctively that they needed good people at all levels of their organization in order to overcome their challenges and to achieve their goals. Unfortunately, few would say that they could find these people already within their organizations.

As I reviewed research study after research study, they all seemed to focus on the importance of how the best organizations thought about and acted towards their people. These organizations actually do put people at the center of all that they do. It may be a cliché, and it might be overused, but the greatest asset an organization really can have is its people. An organization's people are the one thing that a competitor can't duplicate. People are what are needed to solve the tough problems and to give that personal touch to a customer. For high performance organizations, it isn't just people, but the best people that they can find. They go out to look not for superstars, but for really good solid performers who can be team players and who are excited about what the organization is doing.

Often you will hear that with the shift to an information economy that people are increasingly becoming more important to the success of the organization. While we have seen an increased focus on people as the information economy becomes more entrenched, I believe that people have always been important, no matter what economy we have been experiencing or what industry your organization is in. If you aren't focusing on people and putting them at the center, then your organization will most likely never perform at consistently high levels over a long period of time.

When talking about people in organizations we often get caught up in just discussing two groups: employees and customers. While both of these groups of people are extremely important to the success of the organization, they are not the only groups of people that we should be concerned with. There are actually seven groups of people, or constituencies, that every organization must interact with, and they must balance the needs of each constituency against the needs of the others. These constituencies are:

Shareholders: The people who own the organization and/or have invested in it. It might be a sole proprietor, partners, a group of investors, stockholders, the board of directors of a non-profit, or the citizens of a government. These are people who are investing time and money into the success of the organization, and often the organization would not exist without them.

Management: The people who the shareholders have chosen to oversee the operations of the organization and to insure success. This group provides the leadership and direction for the organization.

Employees: The people who management hires to do the work of the organization.

Customers: The people who receive goods and services from the organization. Without these people the organization would have no need to exist.

Strategic Partners: The people who the organization interacts with in order to deliver goods and services to their customers. These are such people as suppliers, transportation and logistics, retailers, distributors, benefits providers, etc.

Government Regulators: The people who belong to the various governmental agencies that might have oversight of the operations of the organization.

The Community: The people who live in and around where the organization exists or does business, and who aren't necessarily a member of any other of the constituencies, but who might be.

A high performing organization understands the needs of each of these constituencies and balances those needs in order to achieve performance. They also understand that there is a network or system that will best achieve the balance between these constituencies for the organization.

In their groundbreaking work first published in a management research journal, and then later in the book *First Break All the Rules*, the Gallup Organization introduced us to the concept of engagement, and, in particular, employee engagement. They shared with us that there are three kinds of employees:

Engaged: Those who are loyal, productive, and find their work satisfying. These employees will do what it takes to make the organization successful.

Unengaged or Not Engaged: Those who are not psychologically committed to their roles. They show up for work, do what they have to do to stay out of trouble, and then go home.

Actively Disengaged: Those who are disenchanted with their workplaces. Often these people hate their job and their employer, and may be actively working to hurt the organization.

The research further revealed that in the average organization that one out of every two employees are unengaged and are only at work to do what they have to do to get by. Often you hear of these people as being referred to as nine-to-fivers. Once in a while they might become engaged for a short time, but with little to reinforce their engaged behavior they quickly slip back to becoming unengaged. When I ask my clients how they would rate these people's performance on a scale of one to ten, most tend to say that they would be performing at a four, five, or maybe even a six. Contrast this performance level with those of engaged employees. When asked the same question, most of my clients are indicating that their best employees are performing at an eight, nine, and even a ten.

This is a huge performance gap. If your organization is average, then half of your employees are working at about half of the performance level that they could be working. When confronted with this thought many are taken aback by the huge gap in performance, and can't believe that they have so many low performers, but in fact, about a quarter of their employees actually are working at that higher level. Now throw on top of this that about one in five of your employees don't like their job or the organization, and as my clients have indicated, are probably performing at a two or a three, then if you are the average organization you are wasting a huge amount of your resources and missing out on lost opportunities to perform. As a result, Gallup estimates that the average organization is essentially throwing away one-third of its payroll in lost opportunity and performance, and my work with my clients seems to support this.

It is no wonder that the best organizations can outperform their closest competitors by such a large margin as 700% to 1500%. We often tend to think that the average is pretty good, and in reality, the average organization is pretty good. But when we see this kind of performance gap, who would ever want to settle for being average? Yet it is clear that so many organizations do settle for mediocrity. Just think of this for a moment; if second best gets you 700% less, how much less does being mediocre (average) get you? Just imagine what you could achieve if you could tap into the potential of your people!

I think one of the biggest reasons that organizations don't leverage their people more is that most organizations really don't understand the concept of engagement, and often confuse it with terms such as satisfaction or employee happiness, and ideas such as "great places to work." While there are some direct links between engagement and concepts such as satisfaction and great places to work, we have to keep in mind that only engagement has a direct correlation to creating high performance.

The research says that if you engage employees then you will see organizational performance increase. You will also probably see an increase in employee satisfaction and you will also probably find that the organization is a great place to work. High performance organizations don't set out with *Intent* to create great places to work or happy or satisfied employees. They set out with *Intent* to create performance by engaging their employees. The rest is simply a by-product of having engaged employees.

Engagement Versus Satisfaction

Satisfaction and engagement are not the same, yet I often hear a lot of people use the two terms interchangeably. When speaking to clients and groups about the concept I often share the following story to explain the two concepts.

A few years ago I received an invitation from an online survey software company to attend a luncheon and a presentation of their product in Jacksonville, Florida. I was interested in their product as a possible solution for a couple of clients, so I responded that I would attend. The event was held in a quaint little bistro on the north side of town. The bistro only served dinner, but was available for rental for lunch for special events. The food at this bistro was excellent, and the service was superb, and I found the entire event highly enjoyable. I was very satisfied with my experience at this establishment.

However, the likelihood that I will ever go back to that establishment is very slim. First, I don't even recall the name of the establishment or exactly where it was located. Second, while attending the session I was thinking that perhaps I could also use the establishment as an opportunity to provide a similar experience for a few potential clients in the Jacksonville area. However, as we were being served it was announced that effective the following week that they would start opening to the public for lunch, so they would not be available for private rental any longer.

Finally, Jacksonville was just over 60 miles away from my home, so driving there for dinner with Ann, my wife, probably wasn't going to happen, even for those rare times we went to Jacksonville to attend the theatre or some other show because the bistro was located in a part of town that wasn't close by our events. So while I was very satisfied with my experience at the bistro, I am just not going to return.

Contrast this with another restaurant establishment, On the Border, in Gainesville, Florida. Now On the Border is a chain of restaurants, but this particular restaurant has become Ann's and my favorite place to go for dinner. Despite Gainesville being close to 40 miles away from our home, we will find an excuse to go to Gainesville for dinner at On the Border about twice a month.

We never sit in the main dinning area, but instead we have a couple of tables that we like to sit at in the bar area. We visit often enough that most of the wait staff in the bar area know us, and when we do get a new waitperson they are quickly told by the others that we are "regulars." As a result, we get exceptional service. The manager, Kyle, often stops by and spends some time with us just talking about a variety of things. It is an easy conversation and an enjoyable evening. We can easily spend a couple of hours there, enjoying the food, atmosphere, and people.

Even today, with us living four hours away from Gainesville, whenever we find that we are going to be back down in the Gainesville area we are quickly making plans to spend some time at our favorite restaurant, On the Border.

This story clearly demonstrates the difference between satisfaction and engagement. The bistro in Jacksonville provided me with good food and service and an enjoyable time, yet while being satisfied I am not engaged with that restaurant. On the other hand, Kyle and his staff at *On the Border* have completely engaged us. We go there whenever we can and are loyal customers. If by some chance we might get a new waitperson that doesn't do such a great job, the rest of the staff always make up for it. If for some reason we might get some improperly prepared food, it is usually taken care of in some way. We are more likely to forgive the problem because we know that it is a rare event.

Kyle and his staff have learned what it takes to engage their customers. They realize that it is more than just satisfying them, because other restaurants can do that. They take the time to go the extra step to find a way to touch the individual customers that come into their establishment. They not only satisfy, they reach the emotions of their customers.

One day, while I was having a quick late lunch at the restaurant, I sat there with Kyle and his regional manager talking about the concept of engagement. The regional manager asked where does engagement start. Just at that time a person came up and asked if the manager was at the table, and Kyle answered yes and stood up. The customer then told Kyle that he had never been in the restaurant before, but his food and service was excellent and that he would definitely be back. Kyle thanked him and the customer left.

I turned to the regional manager and told him, "That is the beginning of engagement." While satisfaction isn't the same as engagement, you can't get people engaged if they aren't satisfied. To capture that engagement you have to reach people's emotions so that they care. Clearly, that customer cared enough to share that they would be back.

I believe that this story demonstrates another difference between satisfaction and engagement. Satisfaction tells you about what happened in the past. Satisfaction is always about an experience in the past, and tells you nothing about the future. Clearly someone might be satisfied but won't act on that satisfaction in the future. My failure to ever go back to the restaurant in Jacksonville is a clear example.

On the other hand, engagement tells you about the future. If people are engaged, customers or employees, then you have an idea about how they will behave in the future. Engaged customers will come back to see you to buy your products or services; engaged employees will work hard for you and take care of your customers. It is no wonder that, along with measuring cash flow, Jack Welch, former CEO of GE, tells us that the other two most important things that organizations can measure are customer and employee engagement. Unfortunately, most organizations are lousy at measuring customer engagement and rarely, if ever, measure employee engagement.

I think it is interesting that the Cherokee word for "organization," *u na do tlv hi* (the "v" is pronounced as a guttural "uh" sound), is the same word that is used to mean "corporation." It is also the same word used to mean "congregation" and it also means "society." After all, an organization is not a soulless entity that exists as a result of a legal document, but instead it really is the people and the systems that the people create within the organization. It is a society, a community of people working together to accomplish a purpose or goal. The Cherokee call this *ga du gi*, which means "working together to achieve a goal." In order to have *ga du gi* then you must have engaged and committed employees who will engage your customers and work well with the other constituents in order for your organization to overcome its challenges and to achieve its goals.

If an organization wants to become high performing then it must find ways to engage their employees and their customers. Satisfaction is not enough. Placing a focus on people is a start, but it won't get you there. It takes the other six of the Seven Elements to build engagement in your employees, customers and other constituents that will allow you to unlock the power of your people in order for your organization to be high performing.

So let us now continue on and take a look at another of the Seven Elements of High Performance.

The Foundational Elements

CHAPTER 3

Build Trust as a Foundation

The Cherokee, along with many other American Indian Nations, believe that all life exists and springs forth from Elohino, or Mother Earth. Elohino provides the circumstances and the environment for which life can exist. Elohino provides the nourishment to sustain us, even in times of trouble. As I studied the research about high performance organizations I quickly saw a relationship between the nurturing environment of Elohino to the concept of Trust in being able to create levels of high performance in an organization. Trust, like Elohino, provides the foundation for all the other Elements to be able to work together to create performance in the organization. Based on this, I have placed Trust in the model in the position of Mother Earth as the foundation for the Model.

The sad thing, though, is that study after study also revealed a horrible lack of Trust in most organizations. There is a huge linkage between lack of Trust in organizations and the low levels of engagement that is present in the average organization. This actually isn't really that amazing. In their book *Now Discover Your Strengths*, Marcus Buckingham and Donald Clifton stated:

> *Our research tells us that the single most important determinant of individual performance is a person's relationship with his or her immediate manager. Without a robust relationship with a manager who sets clear expectations, knows you, trusts you and invests in you, you are less likely to stay and perform.*

If People are the key to having a successful, high performance organization, then it does take a strong, positive relationship with those people that will enable them to perform. The basis of all relationships is Trust. What I have found, however, is that when I tend to talk about Trust with managers is that they talk about Trust from their point of view, not their employees' or their customers' points of view. We have to understand that things change based on whose points of view we are looking at things from.

Trust is something that one person gives to another. It is a very personal thing and is very much emotional. While some might try to apply logic to explain why they do or don't Trust someone, Trust is still founded in their emotions. Often someone might even say, "I don't know why, but I just don't trust that person." Because Trust is something that one person gives to another and is based on their emotions, there is just nothing that you can do to *make* someone Trust you. Yet, oftentimes managers try.

> *I was working with a client and I learned of a situation that had happened a few months before that had caused a lot of problems for*

them. This was a professional services organization that operated in an office setting. Most of the employees were professionals, and many of them had college degrees. Each employee worked on their own schedule and set their own appointments with the customers that they served. The standard hours of work were from 8:00 am until 5:00 pm.

It seems that there were a couple of people who were showing up late to work in the mornings on a regular basis in one of the offices. The office manager decided to do something about it. However, instead of addressing the issue with the couple of employees that were late, the manager imposed a new set of rules on the entire office. Effective immediately, each employee was supposed to send an e-mail to their supervisor upon arriving to work each morning, and those e-mails should be sent before 8:00 am or that employee might face disciplinary action.

If we analyze this story we can learn a lot of different lessons. One lesson might be about the focus on time rather than on accomplishing work. After all, just because an employee sends the e-mail before 8:00 am doesn't mean that they are working. They could easily arrive in their office in time to send the e-mail before 8:00 am and then go wandering off to the employee lounge or kitchen area to grab a cup of coffee, stop to chat with co-workers on the way back, and then sit at their desk reading a newspaper until 8:30 or 9:00 a.m. Being on time to work does not mean that someone will actually be productive.

However, in relation to Trust, what we see is that the office manager was having a problem with some employees' behaviors that were causing the manager to not Trust them. When the manager set out to deal with the situation they were acting from their point of view. They took action based on that point of view thinking that they were looking out for the organization's best interests. This manager thought that they were being Trustworthy by taking this action to protect those interests of the organization.

While earning Trust is from the point of view of the other person, being Trustworthy is from our own point of view. We do things that we think will earn Trust or we ask others to do things to earn our Trust. But being Trustworthy is not the same thing as Trust. We can act on our own beliefs and be as Trustworthy as we believe we can be, yet still fail to earn the Trust of someone else.

In the example above, while the manager made their staff act in what they thought was a Trustworthy manner (be to work by 8:00 a.m. and send an e-mail to that effect), this behavior did nothing to help the employees Trust the manager or the manager to Trust their employees any more. In fact, if anything, this action by the manager, no matter how well meaning and intentioned and focused on being Trustworthy it was, probably did more to destroy Trust than create Trust. What this action told the employees is that the manager did not Trust them, even if they were already showing up to work on time.

If having Trust in an organization is essential to having high performance, and if we can't make others Trust us, and if being Trustworthy doesn't always produce Trust, then what must we do to have Trust in our organization? Simply put, we must Build Trust. While Trust is something someone else gives to us, and being Trustworthy is something we decide about ourselves or others, building Trust is something we do as an interactive set of behaviors with someone else.

If the research says that an employee's performance is based on the relationship that they have with their manager, then Trust Building is the behaviors that promote positive relationships which leads to engaged employees. There are fFour bBehaviors that bBuild Trust™ and they are:

Straightforwardness — Saying what needs to be said in a non-threatening and non-judgmental manner. Conflicts are faced, not avoided.

Openness — A willingness to listen to others about issues. Encouraging others to speak up, as well as sharing our own ideas, thoughts, and feelings. Differences of opinion are sought and valued.

Acceptance — Appreciating others who are different in behavioral styles, approaches, and appearances. We appreciate people for the strengths, experiences, and expertise that they bring to the organization.

Reliability — Will follow through on or do what was said or promised would be done at a high level of quality.

Notice that the Four Behaviors that Build Trust™ are just that; behaviors. They are not ideals, beliefs, or wishes. These are things that you must do, not hope will happen. But like anything else, the specific behaviors that will exemplify Straightforwardness, Openness, Acceptance, and Reliability will depend on your organization and the point of view of the individual. It is why it is so important to discuss these behaviors within the organization and identify specific examples of each that build and support them, as well as the kinds of specific examples of behaviors that will destroy each of them.

When I am working with managers of an organization in a group I will have them answer a series of questions regarding each of the Four Behaviors that Build Trust™. Then I ask them to share with the group some specific examples of behaviors that would exemplify each of the Behaviors that Build Trust™. I then ask them to identify examples of behaviors that would destroy Trust. Their homework for that session is to have a meeting with thosetheir employees who report directly to them directly so that they can share about the Four Behaviors that Build Trust™. They then talk with their team about examples of behaviors that build and examples of behaviors that destroy Trust.

This exercise accomplishes a couple of things. First, it gets everyone focusing on what it takes to achieve high levels of Trust in an organization. Second, it allows everyone to accurately define through specific examples what is and isn't acceptable behavior for their group and their organization. Finally, it begins to open dialogue about Trust, but it also helps to open up lines of communication about all sorts of issues in the organization. It allows employees to clear the air about issues from the past, as well as talk about what is important to them in accomplishing their work.

> *"The past is the past. Let it be." The self-destruction that occurs through guilt or blame takes one out of harmony and balance, though these things, too, offer important lessons. However, once something is done, it is done. And all you can do is the best you can do at the point in time given what you have available to you. So once something has happened, all you can do is the best you can do from that point on, which also may mean having an opportunity to correct or compensate for, as is the traditional Cherokee Way, wrongs committed in order to restore the balance and peace.*
>
> *The past is the past. And yet, regardless, it is also very much alive in our hearts. It is very much a part of who we are. For who are we but the culmination of all of our experiences and memories and perceptions?*
>
> MICHAEL GARRETT
> *WALKING ON THE WIND*

When I work with organizations I rarely work directly with the employees. Instead, I focus my efforts on management, allowing them to work with and build relationships with their employees. My feeling is that if I work with their employees then I will be the one building the relationship with them, and that isn't the goal of my work. However, in one organization that I was working with I happened to know one of the employees from another organization I was involved with. One day I happened to encounter her and we started talking about some things that were happening in her organization. She told me that when things first started that she had her doubts about how much impact our consulting would have on her organization. Then her workgroup had their conversations with her manager. They were able to talk about some issues that went way back; some things happening over ten years ago! Yet, for her the past was very much alive in her heart and it was causing problems with Trust in the organization. As a result of the conversations that the team was having with the manager she was able to deal with it and talk with her manager to resolve the issues and to begin Building Trust. She was now reenergized and excited about her work and the possibilities that lay ahead.

It isn't until we can begin talking about issues of the past, not to lay blame but to resolve those issues so we can put them to rest, will the organization be able to move forward with its Trust building efforts. As we open lines of communication we can learn how to be Straightforward, Open, Accepting, and Reliable because we learn how to define them in the context of our organization and our own workgroups. As we define and talk about the Four Behaviors that Build Trust we learn how to let the past be and achieve balance for ourselves and those we work with.

Something else that I have discovered through my own experience in working with organizations to Build Trust is that there is one of the Behaviors that Build Trust that is a key to unlocking all of the others. This became glaringly apparent to me as I worked with an intact team of professionals at a major university. As we were doing some of the exercises on Trust Building they were sharing their answers to the questions "What kinds of people do you feel most accepting of?" And, "What kinds of people are you least accepting of?" They had been given some time to think about and write down their own answers, and then we went around the table of about a dozen team members.

Almost to a person I tended to hear from them that they were most accepting of other people who were also accepting, and that they were least accepting of other people who tended to be closed and not accepting of others. While I had received similar answers prior to my work with them, and continue to hear similar answers, it was the way this group phrased their answers so similarly that caused me to take notice. Afterwards, I pondered the importance of what they had shared and it became apparent that Acceptance is the key to unlocking the Four Behaviors that Build Trust™.

If we are not accepting of others, if we don't value them as individuals and for the strengths, experiences, and expertise that they can provide to the team and the organization, then we are less likely to be Straightforward with them, and if we are, then we certainly won't be Straightforward in such a way as to be non-threatening and non-judgmental. This means that we will not share what we think is important with others for fear of hurting others feelings. Or, if we do share, then we might tend to do so in a way that will only harm the relationship and end up destroying Trust. Telling someone something "for their own good" in a harsh and unfeeling way will not build a positive relationship with that person.

If we are not accepting of others then we are also less likely to have openness in our organization. People will not share their ideas if they do not believe that they are valued as individuals first. An example of this is when I was talking with a friend who was not feeling very appreciated in her organization. She felt that she wasn't valued for what she could bring to the organization and often felt ignored by her manager. In essence, this person didn't feel like she was accepted by either her manager or others higher up in the organization. My friend also shared with me that she had been to a meeting with another organization. They had some ideas about some things that her organization could do to take advantage of a particular situation. My friend then said "But I'll be damned if I'll share that with anyone. If they don't care about me then why should I care about them?"

Granted, this could be self-destructing behavior on the part of my friend, and I actually believe it is, but this also demonstrates the emotional side of Trust. When people don't feel trusted they often react in an emotional and non-logical manner, resulting in behaviors (or lack of behaviors in this case) that can hurt them and the organization over the long-term.

Finally, if we are not accepting of others then we are also less likely to be reliable with them. It is all too easy to dismiss commitments that we make to others if we don't accept and value them. It then becomes easy to justify missing a deadline or failing to follow-up on a promise if that person isn't that important to us.

In essence, Acceptance is all about letting someone know that they are valued; that they are important to the organization and that what they do has meaning. In the previous chapter I talked about the research by Gallup regarding engaged, unengaged, and actively disengaged employees. We gain engaged employees when they believe that what they do is important and worthwhile to the success of the organization. We gain unengaged employees when they feel that they are not accepted and valued by the organization. We gain actively disengaged employees when this feeling of not being accepted is intensified.

If we want to increase acceptance in our organization, on our team, or just increase our own ability to be accepting of others, then there is a very simple model we can turn to in order to help us.

Knowledge

Understanding

Acceptance

Behavior

The more we know about other people the better we will understand them; the better we understand them the more likely we will accept them for who they are; the more we accept people for who they are then we will change our behaviors towards them. The change in behaviors are the behaviors that surround Straightforwardness, Openness, and Reliability. As stated before, performance is predicated on the relationships that employees have with their managers. How, then, can you have a relationship with someone who you don't know that much about, who you don't understand, and who you don't accept? Knowledge, therefore, is our starting point. We have to start talking with those we want to Build Trust with so that we can learn more about them and what is important to them.

Building Trust is not easy; in fact, it is downright hard. While my clients have found that having conversations with their employees about the Four Behaviors that Build Trust™ makes things easy, they still find it hard to change some of their notions surrounding the importance of being Trustworthy at the expense of building Trust. We either Build Trust or we Destroy Trust and being Trustworthy could cause either, as we saw in the story of the e-mails. This means that when we make decisions about problems, people's behaviors, policies, courses of action, or just about anything else in our organization, we have to ask ourselves just how does the decision support the Four Behaviors that Build Trust™. Are we possibly trying to be Trustworthy at the expense of building Trust?

It takes a long time to Build Trust in an organization. That same Trust can be lost in a moment through a single careless, thoughtless action. We can all make mistakes, but it is crucial to use the Four Behaviors that Build Trust™ to continue to Build Trust, even in the face of a mistake. All it takes is being Straightforward and Open in acknowledging that we have made a mistake and ask for help from others who we broke Trust with in order to be able to learn and move forward (Openness and Acceptance) so that the mistake will not happen again (Reliability). Just as my wife and I would forgive the occasional problem with our food order at our favorite restaurant, most employees will forgive that occasional lapse in judgment *if* we are willing to own up to it and try to make amends.

Conversely, if we have those who consistently behave in ways that Destroys Trust, then action must be taken. People who Destroy Trust can't stay. Let me say that again. ***People who Destroy Trust can't stay***. I have been sharing that one simple concept with clients and others for several years now. You don't punish people for making mistakes, as mistakes help us learn. You don't punish people for things that go wrong that are part of the system. You don't punish people for things that go wrong when they had no decision in the matter. In essence, you don't punish people, period. If you want engaged people then you don't use punishment at all.

However, when people make conscious decisions to exhibit behaviors that Destroy Trust, and are not willing to make amends and change their behavior, then they must be asked to leave the organization. Banishment has long been a part of the American Indian justice system. The goal of accomplishing justice should always be to regain balance in society and all that are involved. If we remember that an organization is a society, then our goal whenever someone makes a mistake is to regain balance and harmony for the organization, not to punish. When people refuse to change their behaviors regarding Trust, then those people must be asked to leave the organization for the sake and goodness of the organization. Failure to get rid of those people who Destroy Trust will in the end only destroy the organization's ability to be high performing, and that just shouldn't be allowed to happen.

No matter how good of a performer a person is, if someone is behaving in such a way as to destroy Straightforwardness, Openness, Acceptance or Reliability, then the organization must act and act swiftly. If one person is allowed to act in a manner to Destroy Trust and the organization does not take immediate action, then the rest of the members of the organization will believe that Trust is no longer important, and they will act accordingly; i.e., in a less than engaged manner.

Of course, if Trust is truly a foundation for an organization, then everyone in the organization is encouraged to share openly and honestly about behaviors that will and won't Build Trust. Employees feel like they have the ability to be Straightforward with anyone, even someone in management above them, about behaviors that they see being exhibited that are contrary to Building Trust. Those people will be open and receptive to this sharing because they know that what is being shared is for the good of the organization. They will then act reliably by making changes in their behaviors, and if they don't, then the rest of the organization will call for them to leave.

Is this being idealistic and over simplistic in the "real world?" I don't think so. I believe that it is very much possible. In fact, the best organizations operate this way. After all, Jack Welch, the former CEO of General Electric is constantly talking about the necessity of candor to organizational success. Candor is just another word for Straightforwardness and Openness tempered with Acceptance and Reliability.

The Central Element, People, says that we have to place our focus on people if our organizations are going to become high performing. Yet the research says that three quarters of our employees aren't engaged and committed to doing their jobs. If we are going to ever release the hidden potential that is trapped within three out of every four of our employees, then we must create an environment of Trust at all levels within our organization. As I said earlier, people who do not feel that they are appreciated, valued, accepted, and trusted aren't going to go that extra mile for you and the organization. If you do not Build Trust throughout your organization then you will not gain engaged employees, which means you will not have engaged employees to engage your customers.

But Trust alone will not create an environment that will allow high performance to flourish in an organization, which leads us on to the next element of the Seven Elements of High Performance™.

The Four Behaviors that Build Trust™

1. **Straightforwardness** – expectations are clear, disagreements are discussed and resolved, individual performance is discussed and agreed upon, and credit is given where credit is due.

    ### Directness
    We are clear about what we mean

    ### Honesty
    We are always truthful and honest

2. **Openness** – employees exchange information, discuss feelings and opinions and do not keep secrets.

    ### Responsiveness
    We are open to feedback and new ideas

    ### Disclosure
    We share our own ideas and opinions

3. **Acceptance** – employees are respected for their contribution, differences are valued and leadership is shared.

    ### Receptiveness
    We value the individual differences in others

    ### Respect
    We value the abilities and contributions of others

4. **Reliability** – employees can count on each other for support, keep their commitments, and strive for excellence in what they do.

    ### Keeps Commitments
    We do what we say

    ### Seeks Excellence
    We do our best in everything we do

The Four Behaviors that Build Trust™ are the property of Resource Development Systems, LLC

CHAPTER 4

Allow Personal Responsibility Through Individual Decision Making

E arlier I shared about a time when some colleagues and I were talking to executives and managers and asking what kinds of people they needed in order to overcome their challenges and achieve their goals. As they shared the attributes of the kinds of employees they needed, in essence they were telling us that they needed employees who were willing to do what it takes to get their job done and were committed to the success of the organization. What they were telling us is that they needed people who would be Personally Responsible.

As I continued my study of research on high performance organizations it became increasingly clear that Personal Responsibility as a concept, not just as a trait in people, was highly important to creating the kind of environment that would allow the organization to tap into the ability of the People in order to perform. As such, it soon found its way into the model that was developing as the second foundational component, or in the position equivalent to Father Sky, or the Sky Vault in the upper part of the model.

Every CEO dreams about having personally responsible people, because they know that those people are the most productive. Yet according to the research we have already looked at, only about a quarter of the employees in the average organization are engaged and acting in a Personally Responsible manner; the rest are just there to do what they have to do to stay out of trouble and get by, or worse, are trying to hurt the organization.

As I delved into this concept of Personal Responsibility I also realized unfortunately, that there was a lot of difference between the concept of Personal Responsibility and how many people defined Personal Responsibility. Unfortunately, too many CEOs and managers do the wrong things to try to increase Personal Responsibility. They use rules and regulations, threats and coercion, basically imposing their will on others. In other words, they are attempting to force employees to be Personally Responsible. Unfortunately, this just doesn't work. People are only Personally Responsible when they choose to be.

Let's face it; when people complain about not having Personally Responsible people what they are often looking for are people who we can blame when things go wrong. After all, what is usually one of the first things you hear people cry when things go wrong? "We need to hold some one responsible for this!" Perhaps they use the word "responsible" or maybe even the word "accountable," but either way, they are talking about finding someone to take the blame and be punished. No wonder there is such a lack of Personally Responsible people to be found! Who would want to be the person to always be blamed and punished when things go wrong for whatever reason? And believe me, the reasons things go wrong are numerous, but rarely is it the fault of people who are intent on making things go wrong. People may make mistakes, but they seldom do things to intentionally hurt the organization.

I shared in the previous chapter about the issue of placing blame and trying to punish people for making mistakes isn't a good way to Build Trust, and, in fact, can actually Destroy Trust. When you seek to blame and punish people for making mistakes it also destroys Personal Responsibility, as well. If you want to have more Personally Responsible people then the first thing you must do is get rid of your culture that places blame on people. Remember, the only people we are going to ask to leave the organization are those that Destroy Trust.

Putting a halt to blame placing is only the first step in achieving a culture that creates an environment for high performance to flourish, but it goes a long ways in overcoming the fears that keep both managers and employees from allowing Personal Responsibility to flourish. I will share more on this concept of fear later, but first I would like to share a story with you that can help us understand more about Personal Responsibility.

> *A friend of mine was at one time the Administrator for the Indian Health Services hospital on a reservation. He had recently been appointed to the position and was very excited to be working back at the reservation where he had grown up as a boy. One day he came across a young physician who was talking very sternly to an elderly Cherokee woman who, in this young doctor's opinion, wasn't doing a good job of taking care of her health. He was berating her and*

talking down to her, telling her what she should be doing. She stood there quietly, not saying a word.

My friend went running up to the young doctor and began yelling at the doctor. "How dare you talk to an elder in that manner!" My friend was quite upset, for you see, elders are held in high regard in American Indian culture. But this doctor was not American Indian, and wasn't aware of the cultural issues. The doctor was at first taken aback by my friend's behavior, then became angry and stormed off, now mad at the administrator.

My friend then turned to the elderly woman and apologized profusely for the doctor's behavior. "Grandmother, I am so sorry for how that doctor behaved towards you. It was atrocious and should never have happened," my friend told her.

The elderly woman quietly and calmly only replied to him "You stole my Personal Power."

My friend was puzzled. "How did I steal your Personal Power?" he asked.

The woman replied, "I had the choice to determine if I was going to become angry at the doctor or not. It was my Personal Power to make that choice; to decide if I was going to retain my Personal Power or give it away to the doctor by becoming angry at him. I chose not to become angry. But when you came up and became angry for me, my choice was gone. You took it from me and became angry for me. You stole my Personal Power and gave it away to the doctor."

My friend finally understood what he had done. By stepping in he had decided how the situation should have been handled, rather than allowing the person who was in the best position to decide to make that decision. He apologized to the woman, and later to the doctor, and learned a valuable lesson.

I have frequently shared this story with my clients and at speaking engagements, and I usually end up asking "So, how often do you make decisions for others, tell them what to do, and steal their Personal Power?"

This concept of Personal Power is tremendously important in understanding the concept of Personal Responsibility. Each and every one of us has our own Personal Power. We can choose to retain it and own our decisions and the reactions to the emotions that we have. I am sure that the elder woman probably had a variety of emotions that she felt as the young doctor chided her about her health. Yet she realized that she had the choice as to how she would behave towards that doctor. She could have become angry and shouted and yelled at the doctor. This would have probably accomplished the same thing that was accomplished when my friend became angry; both sides storming off with both believing that the other was to blame (there's that "blame" word again).

The elderly woman could have then justified her actions by saying that the young doctor had "made" her angry by his actions. If she had, then this would be where she would have given her Personal Power away to the doctor. No one can "make" us do anything. We all have the choice to do something or not do something. Often we give that choice away and say that others "made" us do something or behave in certain ways. Of course, this isn't being Personally Responsible.

A lack of Personal Responsibility happens when people, managers, employees, customers, and others, chose to relinquish their Personal Power to others. This can come in one of two ways: either they choose to give away their Personal Power to others by allowing them to make decisions for them; or, they have their Personal Power stolen from them, much like the elder woman in the story above, by others who make decisions for them. Either way, the person is not the one who makes decisions about what should or shouldn't be done; others make those decisions for them, and usually it is management.

If the person gave away their Personal Power they will most likely comply with the decision, as they don't want to be blamed if things go wrong. Their attitude is that they avoid blame because they didn't make the decision; someone else did. Their feeling is that they are not responsible for the success or the failure of the decision and the ensuing course of action.

If the person wanted to make the decision but someone else made the decision for them, then they will feel like they had their Personal Power stolen from them, much like the elder woman. Oftentimes these people will resist those decisions and they have an attitude of resentment towards those who made the decision. In the end, they still feel like they are not responsible for the outcome of the decision, because, after all, they didn't get to decide.

Whether the person gave away their Personal Power or they had it stolen, in both instances they have no investment in the outcome of the decision and don't really care if it is successful or not. Neither of these people are Personally Responsible, and because they haven't been involved in making the decision then they won't be. They just did what they were told to do. Their mindset is one of "I have to," not one of accepting Personal Responsibility.

In the end this leads us to the unengaged and actively disengaged employees that we have been discussing, which makes up about three-quarters of the average organization's employees. What you get in the end with those who complied are unengaged employees, doing just what they have to do to get by. Those who resist become actively disengaged with the organization, causing severe problems, and undermining all the hard work that your engaged, Personally Responsible employees are producing.

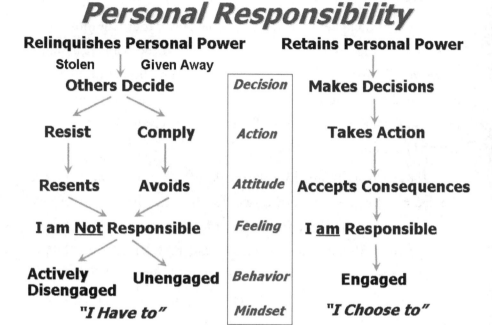

Personal Responsibility

Relinquishes Personal Power			Retains Personal Power
Stolen	Given Away		
Others Decide		*Decision*	Makes Decisions
Resist	Comply	*Action*	Takes Action
Resents	Avoids	*Attitude*	Accepts Consequences
I am **Not** Responsible		*Feeling*	I **am** Responsible
Actively Disengaged	Unengaged	*Behavior*	Engaged
"I Have to"		*Mindset*	"I Choose to"

Contrast this with the employees that decide to retain their Personal Power. These employees make their own decisions. They decide to either agree or disagree about what needs to be done, but they make a decision and they then take action. Their attitude is that they will accept the consequences. As a result, they feel that they are responsible for the outcome, and they have a vested interest to insure that the outcome is a positive one. They behave in ways that show that they are engaged in their jobs, and in the success of the organization. Their mindset towards their managers and the organization is that they get to choose to do the things they do.

Think about the best employees in your organization. Isn't this how they operate? When you think about people who are willing to be Personally Responsible, aren't they the ones who act like it was their choice to do what was done? Don't they go that extra mile to do everything in their power to make things successful? Isn't this the kind of employee you want and need in order to overcome the challenges your organization faces and achieve your goals?

Unfortunately, the average organization only has one in four of their employees willing to choose to retain their Personal Power and be Personally Responsible. If you want to be a high performance organization then you must have a higher concentration of Personally Responsible employees. So where do you find them?

They are already working for you. That's right; those employees who are not being Personally Responsible can become Personally Responsible. All any organization has to do is change some behaviors by management. Management must stop making decisions for employees and allow them to make decisions for themselves. This is scary for many managers and many employees. This is where the fear that I mentioned earlier comes in.

First, employees fear that they do not have the necessary skills and information to make good decisions. In most organizations this might be true, especially when it comes to having the information necessary to make good decisions. Too often we hold back information, believing that information is power. But information is only power for the organization if it is unleashed and shared, and then used to make good decisions that will move the organization forward. After all, those who hold and horde information are not hording power, but actually Destroying Trust by not practicing Openness.

Because employees often don't have the information or sometimes the skills to make good decisions, they then fear that they will be blamed if they make a decision and things go wrong because of this lack of information and skills. After all, being blamed is the largest fear that many employees have and why so many are willing to give away their Personal Power to their managers. If they don't have to make decisions then they can't be blamed when things go wrong. Again, in many organizations this fear is well founded. Too often we want to blame people for things that go wrong rather than learning about the systems, processes, and information that led to the wrong decision.

Either of these fears can be overcome by opening up the lines of information within the organization. If you are Building Trust then this should be easy. The communication that you are engaging in to Build Trust will help you in the exchange of information that will help people make good decisions and move your organization forward.

Employees aren't the only ones that have fears. Managers are afraid to allow employees to make their own decisions for a variety of reasons. First, managers fear that employees will make bad decisions and end up hurting the organization. While there are some employees that might want to hurt the organization (think "actively disengaged" here), most employees really don't want to do things that will hurt the organization, their coworkers, or themselves. The key is to insure that your employees have the training, skills, and information to make good decisions. When they don't make good decisions, don't blame them, but use those moments as a learning opportunity so they can make better decisions next time.

Will employees make mistakes and bad decisions? I'm sure they will. This leads us to the second fear that managers have, and that is a fear of not being needed. After all, if managers don't have to make decisions any more, then what are they supposed to do and why are they needed? The answer, of course, is that managers are needed to help insure that employees have good information and to coach them in making good decisions about their jobs.

All of these fears can be overcome through Trust Building. Trust Building gives both employees and managers the mindset to "choose to" make the decisions that need to be made at the levels where they need to be made. It allows everyone to share information and to believe in and value other's input. Finally, most of all, it gives people faith in others so that they can allow others to make decisions and to take Personal Responsibility. Managers no longer have a need to control things or people, but allow everyone to contribute to helping the organization be successful and high performing.

The Rule of Acceptance teaches us about the importance of listening and opening up our spirits by giving away the need to control or change other people, the need to control things, or the need to control situations. These things remove us from the harmony and balance of the Circle, and just make life difficult when it does not have to be.

MICHAEL GARRETT
WALKING ON THE WIND

But what about those decisions that must be made by managers at higher levels in the organization, or do we allow employees to make all of the decisions? Of course, the answer is no. Employees don't make all of the decisions, but they do make the decisions about how they do their jobs. In regard to the decisions that need to be made at a higher level, we still want them to have input into those decisions. If they can have a say, and if management really listens to them, then they will more readily buy into the final decision and help insure that it is successful and take responsibility for that success.

In working with one of my clients, a small social services organization, I was helping them to focus on a single goal to work on for the next six months or so. The senior team chose the goal and worked to refine it, and then they shared it with their managers to get their buy-in. While the line managers weren't able to make the final decision about the goal that was chosen, they did get to supply input about it. As a result, some changes were made in the goal, and the managers were excited about getting to talk with their staff about the goal and what it would mean to them.

I was talking with the managers afterwards, and I asked them how they felt about the goal and the process. Most shared that they were very excited, not just about the goal, but the fact that they were listened to by the senior team. I asked them how they knew that they were heard, and among other things such as body language, they said that it was because "they made changes based on our suggestions."

This simple act built Trust and Personal Responsibility, as well as engaging these managers and creating a greater likelihood that they will cascade this engagement down to their own staff and throughout the organization. If you want engaged employees then you have to include them in the decision-making process. When people are included they take ownership, and that is Personal Responsibility.

To recap: the lessons that we have learned so far from the Medicine Wheel is that the first step to creating high performance is to put People at the Center. We need highly committed and engaged employees for us to be able to overcome the challenges that our organization faces and to achieve our goals. In order to do this we must create an environment where these People can excel and drive organizational performance. We create this environment by Building Trust and allowing Personal Responsibility through individual decision-making. Without Trust and without people being able to be involved in making the decisions that surround their job then we will not have the kinds of people we need in order to succeed.

It doesn't matter how many Personally Responsible people we hire. If the environment will not allow them to be Personally Responsible: if the environment doesn't allow them to feel trusted: then the best of your employees will just leave. At worst, they will stay but stop being Personally Responsible and become compliant or even worse, actively disengaged.

Having an environment of Trust and Personal Responsibility, while going a long ways in helping your organization to perform, won't get you there on its own. There are four more elements of the Seven Elements of High Performance remaining to be shared.

The Cardinal Elements

CHAPTER 5

Share a Vision of an Aligned Purpose, Values, and Goals

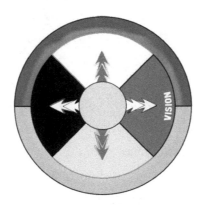

Very early in my research I quickly learned that what passed for creating a "vision" in most companies was pretty worthless in helping to drive high levels of organizational performance. Fancy vision, mission, and values statements just didn't help organizations perform. This is primarily because most organizations created the statements as an exercise in themselves, and then once created the statements became artwork that was hung on walls, but not incorporated into the operations of the organization.

This is evidenced by one of the "shattered myths" from the long-term research conducted by Jim Collins and Jerry Porras that looked at some of the most successful organizations over a performance span of a minimum of 50 years and upwards to over 150 years.

Shattered Myths

Myth 12: *Companies become visionary primarily through "vision statements."*

Reality: *Visionary Companies attained their stature not because they made visionary pronouncements, but because they succeeded in having their core values and purpose permeate the entire organization.*

JIM COLLINS AND JERRY PORRAS

BUILT TO LAST

As I continued to research what makes a difference in performance the concepts of vision, purpose, and values continued to be intertwined in helping to drive performance, but I was beginning to see some differences in how the best organizations approached them verses how the rest of the organizations handled them. Yet, I still struggled to figure out just how all the research fit together in this regard. To be honest, this was one of the latter elements to come together for me. It wasn't until after I had discovered the link to the Medicine Wheel that I was finally able to make sense of it all.

The East, the location in the Medicine Wheel where Vision resides, is the direction of the Spiritual. If Vision is the Spirit of the organization, then how does it work, and how does purpose and values fit in with it? As I wrestled with these questions I also realized that there was another component that had been missing, and that was the way the best organizations approached their goals, and it finally all came together.

Vision then became the combination of the organization's Purpose, Values, and Goals. In other words, an organization's Vision is all about its Purpose and why it exists, the Values it will live by, and the Goals it is going to accomplish while it is in existence. After all, isn't this what Spirituality is for most people; seeking to answer the questions of why we exist, how we will live our lives, and what we will accomplish with our lives? The same is true for the best organizations.

The best organizations add one more thing to these simple concepts. They insure that their Purpose, Values and Goals are all aligned. This alignment is not just with each other, which, of course, is highly important in itself. They also insure that the alignment is cascaded down through the entire organization. They make sure that each person at each level understands just what the Vision means to them.

Before we go any further in talking about Vision, let's first take a look at each of the components of it and then we can look at it as a whole.

Purpose Answers Why

Raccoon and Beaver

Raccoon is a jolly fellow as he wanders along the woods, checking everything out. He moves from the flowers, to the brambles, to the rocks, and to the streams, sniffing and marveling at the wonders of Mother Earth. As he comes across a berry he pops it into his mouth, giving thanks, and then takes a second one and slips it into his pouch that he has around his neck. For you see, you will never know when you might want a snack or find a friend to share with. And as he wanders along he sings his little song: "To-da-la-do, to-da-la-de, the hardest job is just to Be."

And so Raccoon ambles along, sniffing and probing into everything, with no place safe from his inquisitive nose. Chasing butterflies, and romping in meadows, Raccoon finally finds himself along side the stream. As he plays among the rocks he slips and falls into the rushing water.

"Help, Help!" he cries. "I can't swim! Someone save me! Help! Help!" Raccoon continues to holler as he rides the water down the stream towards Beaver's dam. Beaver, working very hard on his damn ignores Raccoon, as he knows perfectly well that raccoons can swim. "Help me Brother Beaver," Raccoon hollers. "Save me from the water!"

"Roll over and stand up," said Beaver gruffly. "The water is not that deep and you know full well that you can swim." Raccoon rolled over and climbed up on a rock with a grin on his face as he shook all over, throwing water all around and into Beaver's face. Beaver shook his own face to get the water out of his eyes and continued "You are lazy, Raccoon, and always distracting others from their work. Winter is coming and you will have no place to live. Now go away and stop bothering me, because I will have a place to live this winter."

Raccoon replied, "But Mother Earth always provides for me. I have no worries about a place to live, as She will provide one. Besides, I know of a tree that has a beehive in it that is dripping with honey. Even Bear doesn't know of this tree. The Bees have more than enough to share and they won't mind if we take some. All you need to do is chew down the tree and we can share the honey and then go off and dance the Friendship Dance. Come on Beaver, let's go get some honey!"

Beaver replied again even more gruffly, "I said NO! I have things to do, so go away and leave me alone!" And with that Beaver swam off to go get more sticks to put in his dam.

Raccoon began to wander off and called over his shoulder, still a grin on his face, "Okay, Beaver, but if you change your mind just holler *for me. I'll be in the woods and will surely hear you." And with that, Raccoon went bounding and crashing off into the woods, still playing and frolicking.*

Beaver continued to pull sticks from the banks of the stream and over to his dam, the whole time muttering angrily to himself about Raccoon. "How dare he! How dare he distract me from my work with useless play! Can't he see that I have so much to do! I must get this dam finished or I'll have no home for this winter!" And with each branch that Beaver brought to the dam, the angrier that he got over the incident with Raccoon.

In fact, he was so angry that he stopped paying attention to things around him, including the rain that had begun. While the rain had started lightly at first, it was now coming down quite heavily. But Beaver paid no attention to it. He was so totally focused on working on and completing his dam, and so thoroughly mad at Raccoon for trying to distract him from his task, that he never noticed the rain or the rising water in the stream. Then all of a sudden, as Beaver was standing in the middle of his dam, there was a great rumble and a flash of lightening. Beaver stopped and looked around and realized that it was pouring down rain.

He again heard another rumble, but this time there was no lightening that preceded it. It was a different sound. Lower and continuous, getting louder and louder, the rumble continued. Then from around the bend in the stream a wall of water came rushing towards Beaver and his dam. Frozen in place, Beaver watched as the wall of water came closer and closer until it hit him and the dam with such a fantastic force that it shook the dam and washed over it and Beaver. The sticks of the dam shifted and some were washed away, and in all of the movement Beaver found his foot wedged down in between the sticks of his dam just where it had washed away.

While the wall of water had swept on and Beaver's head was above water now, he was still stuck and unable to get his foot free. Now the water in the stream was rising up higher and higher, already up to his neck. Beaver began to holler for help, hoping that anyone would hear him and come to his rescue before the stream rose to totally engulf him.

In the woods, Raccoon was still frolicking along, slipping from under this bush to the next to keep as dry as possible in the rain. All of a sudden he heard cries for help. He paused and listened. "That sounds like my friend, Beaver. He's in trouble!" And with that he went bounding through the woods to the stream. Arriving at the edge of the stream Raccoon saw Beaver out in the middle, out just beyond where his dam disappeared into the ever rising and fast rushing stream, his head just barely above the water.

With out a second's thought, Raccoon went bounding out along the top of the dam that was still there until he reached Beaver. Taking a deep breath he dove under the water to pull and yank on the sticks that trapped Beaver's foot. All of a sudden, just as the water was about to rise over Beaver's head, Raccoon freed Beaver's foot and they both found themselves scampering along the dam as it began to be washed away by the rushing water.

Finally reaching the bank of the stream, both shook furiously to rid their fur of the water that drenched their hides. Then they both lay down and catching their breath, Beaver managed to gasp out, "Raccoon, you have saved my life!" Raccoon just grinned and opened his pouch and pulled out a couple of plump blackberries and handed one to Beaver. Both enjoyed the afternoon snack as the rain stopped and Grandfather Sun began to shine again from behind the clouds. They lay in the sunlight and dried off, enjoying the warmth of Grandfather Sun.

Later they went off to frolic in the woods, and eventually they did find that honey tree and shared the sweet nectar and danced the Friendship Dance. To this day, Raccoon and Beaver are fast friends, and call each other "Brother." And if you are careful and quiet, you can slip off into the woods in the autumn and listen; you will hear Raccoon and Beaver dancing the Friendship Dance and singing Beaver's song.

The hardest job is just to Be!

Like most traditional Cherokee stories, the story of Raccoon and Beaver can provide us with many lessons. However, the primary lesson I would like to focus on at this time comes from the very end of the story – "the hardest job *is* just to Be." Yet, the best organizations seem to have been able to tackle that job. They know not only what they want to do, but they know **why** their organization exists *beyond just making money*. They take the time to learn how to just Be.

If you will recall, organizations that are high performing have highly engaged employees. These employees are committed to accomplishing the goals of the organization and want to see the organization be successful. But why are these employees so committed? Is it because the organizations they work for make a lot of money and then pay them a lot of money? Actually, the research seems to indicate that while the best organizations might pay their employees better than the average, often they are not the highest paying employers. When interviewed about their commitment, employees indicate that money isn't the driving force behind their commitment. To be sure, a certain level of monetary reward has to be present, but the money, itself, isn't what takes them to the next level.

So if it isn't money, what is it? Simply, it is that the employees feel that the work they are doing is important and makes a difference. This is directly related to the Purpose of the organization. If the organization doesn't exist for a greater Purpose other than to just make money then it will not inspire a greater number of employees to give that extra commitment to the organization, and it won't end up being high performing. Purpose tells everyone why they are working hard for the organization and how each person can contribute to the overall success of the organization. Purpose helps people feel that they are important and that their work is important.

Contrast the concept of Purpose to a mission statement. Often mission statements are crafted around what the organization wants to accomplish, and it is often worded from the point of view of management and shareholders and what is important to them. They are often verbose and convoluted, containing all sorts of fancy, yet worthless words. Most employees can't tell you about the mission statement, let alone recite it. Why? Because it isn't inspiring! At least, it isn't inspiring to the employees.

Purpose, on the other hand, should be, and must be, important to everyone that is involved; not just managers and shareholders, but definitely employees, and it should be important to customers, as well. When you first answer the question of "why the organization exists," you then give an enduring focus to everyone connected with the organization.

Values Answer How

Many organizations have values statements. While they might have used a variety of methods to craft them, often the methods involved choosing value statements that they thought might be important or that they thought they should focus on. In essence, those values statements were chosen because people thought those values *should* be important, but had no idea if they really were important to the success of the organization.

As a result, the values statements get printed on a poster and hung on a wall, and maybe printed on wallet cards and tucked away in pockets. They rarely get read, and they are rarely consulted. What was originally thought of as being important ends up becoming marginalized and insignificant. No wonder so many executives and managers think the exercise of creating values statements is a waste of time; for most organizations it really is.

Yet, Values are important to the ability of an organization to become high performing. If Purpose tells us *why* we are doing the work we are doing, then Values tell us *how* we will go about doing that work. Values provide us with the guidelines for our behavior and allow us to make decisions, both day-to-day and long-term strategic decisions. Values aren't something that is placed on the wall or in pockets, but are behaviors we exhibit every day.

To get these kinds of Values, the kind that are useful and not just art, we have to start from a different place to discover them. We have to start with our Purpose and then think about what kinds of behaviors we will have to live in order to be successful in achieving that Purpose. As we work through this exercise, as opposed to the one where we identify ideals that we like, we will discover four to six Values that are unique to that organization and that are necessary for that organization to achieve its unique Purpose.

Now these Values can be internalized and conversations can begin, much like the conversations regarding the Four Behaviors that Build Trust, where managers and team members talk about the kinds of behaviors that exemplify those Values and the kinds of behaviors that would violate those Values. Instead of being art on the wall, the Values are now in a position to actually guide decisions because before any decision is made the decision will be held up against the Values to determine if it will support those Values.

I have a friend who works for a company that has done a lot of work on establishing Values that are lived on a day-to-day basis. Employees are often heard discussing the Values when working in teams to solve problems, deal with issues, and make decisions. When someone violates a Value, employees are quick to call them on it, often dealing with it at their own level, but not hesitating to take the issue to management. My friend, a manager, shared that employees will come into a manager's office and share that some action is wrong because it doesn't support their values; the employee's and the organization's. This is an extremely powerful advantage for this organization. It helps to engage the employees and keep them engaged; at least as long as the organization continues to live the Values and keep them alive.

Goals Answer What

In Chapter 1, I mentioned that one of the reasons most organizations fail to become high performers is that they have failed to identify what performance means for their organization. Too many organizations have goals that are too short-termed and only focused on financial issues. Because they haven't indentified their organization's Purpose, they don't know what they need to do over a long period of time in order to be successful.

Their goals are not enduring and they don't provide direction for their employees. Because goals or the way the goals are measured are constantly changing, they don't provide benchmarks to employees or a scorecard to help them figure out just how well they are doing at helping the organization perform.

High performance organizations, on the other hand, have a set of longer-term Goals and sets of measures that do provide that long-term focus and help to get employees inspired. These Goals are directly related to the Purpose of the organization; things that don't support the Purpose are quickly identified and are no longer pursued. Goals are consistent and provide a sense of stability in an ever-changing world.

While you might approach goal setting in a variety of different ways, I happen to like a variation of the Balanced Scorecard approach. The Balanced Scorecard was developed at the Harvard Business School in 1992 by Robert S. Kaplan and David P. Norton as a strategic planning tool for organizations. It helps organizations focus on creating long-term goals that will not only produce financial returns, but also to help insure longevity of the organization. They approach the goals from four perspectives: from the financial; from the customer; from the internal operations; and from the development of the organization. Later, Kaplan and Norton created a relationship between the four areas of goals and called the graphical representation of the linkages Strategy Maps. For those organizations that were for-profit businesses they tended to put the financial goals at the top. For other organizations, they tended to put customers at the top of the strategy map.

In the Balanced Scorecard approach, Goals have four components:

Objective: This is the major thing to be accomplished. For example, we might say that an objective is to be profitable, retain employees, or to reduce total cycle time.

Measure: This is the observable parameters that will be used to measure progress toward reaching the objective. For example, the objective of profitable growth might be measured by growth in net margin.

Target: The specific target values for the measures. For example, you may set a target of a 7% annual decline in manufacturing disruptions. While the objective and the measure are relatively unchanging, the target may fluctuate from time to time as determined by the organization.

Initiative: Projects or programs to be initiated in order to meet the objective. Again, these initiatives might change based on the needs of the organization and the business environment.

Using these parameters Goals now become enduring, providing stability for the organization. Because what we are measuring and how we are measuring it remains stable, employees now understand what is important to the organization and can better figure out what they need to do in order to achieve the organizations' Goals. Recall that I mentioned earlier that in most organizations 51% of the employees do not know what they need to do in order to help the organization to accomplish its goals, and only 15% could even identify what the organization's top goals were. When we create long-term goals that are stable then it is far easier to communicate to everyone what those goals are and how they can contribute to their achievement.

While I like the approach of Balanced Scorecards and Strategy Maps, we must keep in mind that the central element of the Seven Elements of High Performance is People and the relationships that we create with them. We should also keep in mind that our Purpose, the very reason for the existence of the organization, is something other than to make money, even for a for-profit business; at least it is if it is going to be high performing. Therefore, I believe that we need to make a slight adjustment in the approach to creating goals. As a result, I have adapted the model to create what I call REAL Goals.

REAL Goals

Relationships: These goals are built around the people we must build relationships with in order to be successful: customers and employees. Rather than just focusing on the customer, I have also included the employee, as our relationships with employees will impact on our ability to have relationships with customers. The focus here should be on finding measures that give the organization information about how well it is engaging these two constituencies. Keep in mind that engagement tells us information about the future, not just the past, so this is a very key area to set goals and measures. Therefore, at a minimum, this area should have at least two objectives: employee engagement and customer engagement.

Economics: While the most successful organizations understand that they exist for reasons other than just to make money, they also understand that the financial stability of the organization is still important. We must set goals in the economic area in order to insure that the organization has the other tools and resources that it needs in order to accomplish its Purpose and Goals. If it is a for-profit company it must have money so that shareholders will want to stay invested and will insure the viability of the organization. A non-profit or governmental agency still must have money in order to provide the resources, such as pay for employees or technology, to achieve its Purpose. At a minimum, this area should have at least one objective: cash flow.

Action-Ability: This area is concerned with the internal operations of the organization and can vary greatly depending on the type of organization (for-profit, non-profit, or government) and the industry that it is in. Issues that should be addressed are process flow, total cycle time, waste, and adherence to governmental regulations.

Longevity: This area concerns the ability of the organization to insure that it will remain in operations for many, many years to come. In the Norton/Kaplan approach they often put employee engagement measures in this area, but as I have already shared, I believe that employee engagement measures are important enough to place at the top in the Relationships area. There are other issues that help to insure the long-term viability of the organization, such as research and development efforts, training of employees, and the long-term development of leaders (succession planning).

Cascading Goals

Using the REAL Goal Approach, most organizations will have between six to twelve major long-term goals. Having more Goals than less is not necessarily better, but should be based on the Purpose of the organization and its needs to accomplish that Purpose. Keep in mind that when you have too many Goals then it is often hard to focus on any of them. Now that the REAL Goals have been established they can then be cascaded throughout the entire organization.

Keep in mind that not every division, department or team will directly impact every single Goal or measure that has been established. While any one person might have an indirect impact on all of the goals, their direct impact will be limited to just a few. This isn't a bad thing as most people can only focus really well on a few things at a time. Our primary aim should be to insure that each employee knows how what they do on a regular basis impacts on one, two, or three measures.

If you will recall from Chapter 1, employees reported that they only spent 49% of their time working on the goals that are important to achieving performance for the organization. This just isn't acceptable. By cascading the REAL Goals of the organization down to each employee, they can spend almost all of their time working on the things that matter most to the organization. If something isn't contributing to the success of the organization then it is much easier to determine and then stop doing those worthless activities.

"Visionary," we learned, does not mean soft and undisciplined. Quite the contrary. Because the visionary companies have such clarity about who they are, what they're all about, and what they're trying to achieve, they tend to not have much room for people unwilling or unsuited to their demanding standards.

JIM COLLINS AND JERRY PORRAS
BUILT TO LAST

Vision Provides Stability; Vision Provides the Spark

As I shared earlier, too often owners, executives, and managers just don't take time out from working *in* their business to work *on* their business. They are totally focused on the Doing, and not the Being side of their organization. Yet, this Being side is essential to taking any organization to the next level.

In an ever-changing world, a Vision of an Aligned Purpose, Values, and Goals provides stability that employees need in order to feel safe and secure while facing the complications that arise from conducting business in a very unstable world. Purpose and Values don't change. Employees can rely that the connection that they have to the Purpose and Values will always be there. Employees can rely on the Goals that they are working towards won't change. The things that they might do to accomplish those Goals might, but the objectives and the measures are stable.

With this stability, the Vision also gives employees something to become excited about. Employees feel good when the work that they do means something. By aligning the Vision down through the entire organization each person feels a connection to the organization and feels that they have a stake in its success. If we want people to be engaged then we need to give them an environment of Trust and Personal Responsibility, but then we have to also make sure that they know that what they do is important and makes a difference. After all, who cares if they get to make a decision if the decision isn't important or won't make a difference? The Vision gives the employee a connection to the organization and helps them understand that they do make a difference.

We can't rely on chance alone for employees to make those connections, and that is where the next element of the Seven Elements of High Performance comes in.

CHAPTER 6

Create Emotional Connections through Leadership

O ne of the things that I have noticed over the past several years that I've been working on this project is just how unbalanced most organizations are in their approach to dealing with people, especially employees. Their focus seems to be concentrated in the northwest of the Medicine Wheel. All they are concerned about is what people know that can be used by the organization and what skills they bring that they can do for the organization. Most organizations will go out of their way to not have to deal with people's emotions or their spirituality. Yet, what the research reveals is that it is precisely these two areas of spirituality (Purpose, Values and Goals) and emotions (engagement) that sets the best organizations so far apart from the average.

If People are at the center of the driving force for high levels of performance in an organization, then it is creating an emotional connection between those people and the organization that is the key to unleashing that force. As I shared at the end of the last chapter, high performing organizations don't leave those emotional connections up to chance. They actively manage those connections and insure that people are emotionally engaged.

They also understand the relationship that managers have with the rest of the constituencies of People. Managers cannot directly impact the engagement levels of customers. It is employees that customers interact with, and only managers when things go wrong and employees don't satisfactorily handle the situation. At that point in time the best you will probably be able to do is make the customer happy, but probably not engage them. If employees are engaged and allowed to service customers, then the employee can engage the customer and insure that they will continue to come back. So what the manager can impact is the employee's engagement level, and this is where the manager should put their efforts towards creating emotional connections.

There is no doubt that there is a lot of research, books, theories, and ideas out there about the roles of managers, the roles of leaders, the definitions of each, and the differences in each. It can almost become dizzying. Let's take a look at some of the more current thoughts.

John Kotter in A Force for Change

Management

1. Planning and Budgeting – establishing detailed steps and timetables for achieving needed results, and then allocating resources to make that happen

2. Organizing and Staffing – establishing some structure for accomplishing plan requirements, staffing that structure

with individuals, delegating responsibility and authority for carrying out the plan, providing policies and procedures to help guide people, and creating methods or systems to monitor implementation

3. Controlling and Problem Solving – monitoring results vs. plan in some detail, identifying deviations, and then planning and organizing to solve these problems

Produces a degree of predictability and order, and has the potential of consistently producing key results expected by various stakeholders (e.g., for customers, always being on time; for stockholders, being on budget).

Leadership

1. Establishing Direction – developing a vision for the future, often the distant future, and strategies for producing the changes needed to achieve the vision

2. Aligning People – communicating the direction by words and deeds to all those whose cooperation may be needed so as to influence the creation of teams and coalitions that understand the vision and strategies, and accept their validity

3. Motivating and Inspiring – energizing people to overcome major political, bureaucratic, and resource barriers to change by satisfying very basic, but often unfulfilled, human needs

Produces change, often to a dramatic degree, and has the potential of producing extremely useful change (e.g., new products that customers want, new approaches to labor relations that help make a firm more competitive).

Marcus Buckingham in *The One Thing You Need to Know*

Management

Serve as intermediaries between the people and the company.

1. Select Good People

2. Define Clear Expectations

3. Make Immediate Praise Constant and Predictable

4. Show Care for Your People

   Discover what is unique about each person and capitalize on it.

Leadership

Rally people towards a better future.

Create Clarity

1. Who Do We Serve?

2. What Is Our Core Strength?

3. What Is Our Core Score?

4. What Actions Can We Take Today?

The Disciplines of Leadership

1. Take Time to Reflect

2. Select Your Heroes with Great Care

3. Practice

Discover what is universal and capitalize on it.

Jim Collins in *Good to Great*

Level 5 - Executive

Builds Enduring Greatness through a paradoxical blend of personal humility and professional will.

Level 4 - Effective Leader

Catalyzes commitment to and vigorous pursuit of a clear and compelling vision, stimulating higher performance standards.

Level 3 - Competent Manager

Organizes people and resources toward the effective and efficient pursuit of pre-determined objectives.

Level 2 - Contributing Team Member

Contributes individual capabilities to the achievement of group objectives and works effectively with others in a group setting.

Level 1 - Highly Capable Individual

Makes productive contributions through talent, knowledge, skills, and good work habits.

James Kouzes and Barry Posner in *The Leadership Challenge*

Effective Leaders do the following five things:

Model the Way

Inspire a Shared Vision

Challenge the Process

Enable Others to Act

Encourage the Heart

Of course, we could spend several hours talking about how all of these and many other models differ. As with my original research, I prefer to focus on what they are all saying that is the same or similar, and how the concepts seem to support each other. What seems to stand out so strongly to me is that being a manager is a position that one holds, but being a leader is a role of that position, and quite possibly the most important role that a manager can undertake. It is only through being a leader that a manager can touch people's emotions and get them engaged with the organization. The difference is not in how we define manager and leader, but in a manager's beliefs about their employees and their relationships with those they lead.

> *Our research tells us that the single most important determinant of individual performance is a person's relationship with his or her immediate manager. Without a robust relationship with a manager who sets clear expectations, knows you, trusts you and invests in you, you are less likely to stay and perform.*
>
> MARCUS BUCKINGHAM AND DONALD O. CLIFTON
> *NOW, DISCOVER YOUR STRENGTHS*

It begins with the manager's beliefs about whether they can or can't trust their employees to do the right thing. If a manager believes that they cannot Trust their employees, then the manager will not allow their employees to make decisions about their work and will steal their employees Personal Power. Instead, the manager will tell their employees what to do and use rules, incentives, and the threat of punishment to get them to do what they want them to do.

Of course, this behavior totally destroys Trust and Personal Responsibility, and employees fail to become engaged. In order to try to force employees to become responsible the manager may try to "fix" the employee by sending them to training or some other developmental activity.

*Several years ago I was in Chicago for a few days working on a project when I received a phone call from an HR manager in South Florida that was trying to find a training program for one of her HR employees. She was particularly asking about our **Adventures in Attitudes** program as she thought that her employee needed to change her attitude. I asked her if she would share with me what was happening and why she thought her employee needed to change her attitude.*

She told me that this employee was new and was handling payroll and that the employee was acting as if everyone was out to get her. The HR manager further shared that as the employee was getting settled into her new job she was reviewing operations and she noticed some practices that were not in accordance with the company's policy. This discrepancy was resulting in an overpayment of overtime. When things were looked into further, it was determined that the employee was indeed correct. This meant that all of the other employees that had previously been receiving large checks from their overtime would see a reduction in the future. They were all upset and they were blaming the new HR employee.

I then mentioned to the HR manager that it wasn't paranoia to think others were angry at you if they really were angry at you and that sending the new HR employee off to training to "fix" her attitude would hardly deal effectively with the situation. I offered to visit with her and her staff upon my return to Florida to help them uncover the real underlying issues and find a solution, but never heard from her again. I have no idea if the employee was ever "fixed" or if she just decided to leave.

This story is a perfect example of how managers so often try to "fix" their employees rather than deal with the underlying issues of problems and utilize their strengths. Managers tend to focus on what is going wrong rather than to recognize what is going right and capitalize on it.

As a result, managers tend to define all of their employees' goals and direct their activities, resulting in a workgroup rather than a team of highly energized employees. When things go wrong everyone shirks responsibility, pointing to others to place the blame; usually blame placing is rampant. Employees end up being conformist and compliant, not willing to take chances for the sake of the organization. These certainly aren't the kinds of people that executives and managers have said that they need in order to overcome their business challenges and achieve their goals that were talked about in Chapter 2.

Manager Authority RELINQUISHED PERSONAL POWER	● ● ● ● ● ● ● ● ● ● ● ● ● ● ● ● ●	Employee Responsibility RETAINED PERSONAL POWER
CAN'T TRUST PEOPLE TO DO THE RIGHT THING	BELIEFS ABOUT PEOPLE	TRUSTS PEOPLE TO DO WHAT'S RIGHT
DIRECTOR	MANAGEMENT STYLE	LEADER
TELLS IN A DIRECTIVE WAY	MANAGER BEHAVIOR	ASKS QUESTIONS TO FIND SOLUTIONS
USES RULES AND INCENTIVES	APPROACH TO MOTIVATION	CREATES PRIDE AND SELF-MOTIVATION
OVERCOME WEAKNESSES & FIXING PEOPLE	PEOPLE DEVELOPMENT	INCREASING STRENGTHS & GROWING PEOPLE
DEFINES GOALS and DIRECTS ACTIVITIES	GOAL SETTING	CREATES EMOTIONAL CONNECTIONS to PURPOSE & GOALS
WORK GROUP or PSEUDO TEAM	TEAM BEHAVIOR	HIGH PERFORMING and SELF-MANAGING
BLAMES OTHERS	RESPONSIBILITY	WELCOMES RESPONSIBILITY
COMPLIANT, CONFORMIST and NON-ADVENTUROUS	PEOPLE NEEDED	OPEN, CREATIVE, PROACTIVE, RESPONSIBLE

The Context Is Established By Our Beliefs About Our Ability to Trust People

Contrast this with the manager that believes that they can Trust their employees to do the right thing. This manager does not steal the Personal Power of their employees, but rather encourages them to make decisions on their own about their work. When problems arise, the manager who is acting as a Leader will not tell employees what to do, but rather ask the right questions to help the employees to discover solutions to the problem. They create pride and self-motivation in the employees and recognizes their strengths and helps them to grow in the areas where they can grow the most. They create an emotional connection between the employee and the organization through the Purpose and Goals that the organization is trying to achieve.

This manager who is acting as a Leader is building a highly developed self-directed work team. They realize that their role is to provide direction through creating those emotional connections to the Purpose, Values, and Goals, and then getting out of the way to let the good employees that the organization has hired do their jobs. These employees are highly responsible because they are encouraged to make their own decisions about their own jobs, and are involved in the decision-making of even more important things higher up in the organization. Their opinions, experience, and expertise are valued. As a result, these people end up being open, creative, proactive, and responsible. These are the kinds of people that the executives and managers in Chapter 2 said that they needed to have to overcome their business challenges and to achieve their goals. Aren't these the same kinds of people that you want to solve the problems in your organization?

As we can see, it all begins with the manager and their beliefs about people. In order to be high performing the manager must first believe that their People are important. They then must Build Trust and Personal Responsibility in their People and then create emotional connections between their People, the organization and their jobs. This is leadership, and it is imperative if you are going to gain engagement. Managers may have many roles in the organizations that they work in, but the role of being a Leader and creating an emotional connection is the absolute most important role that a manager has. If a manager is failing to engage their employees, then the manager is failing at their job. With each manager that fails at his or her job, the less likely the organization will become high performing.

It is no wonder that so many organizations fail to achieve high performance and are stuck with being mediocre. Managers are rarely taught or trained how to engage employees. What they are trained to do is to enforce rules and regulations, to set goals and directions for employees, and to fix employee's weaknesses. They are taught how to do all the things that lead to unengaged and non-responsible employees. Instead, managers must focus on creating the kinds of relationships that engage employee by creating the environments that Build Trust and Personal Responsibility. Instead of being a director and a controller, they must become a coach and a guide.

Connections, Not "Touchy-feely"

I have heard it on more than one occasion the objections of managers that don't want to get involved in dealing with emotions. After all, for some people, emotions are messy and just "get in the way." But as we talked about in Chapter 2, engagement is all about passion; it is all about caring about what happens in and to the organization. Different people overtly exhibit this passion in different ways. Some people might be more outward and excited about what they do, while others might be less animated and display less enthusiasm, yet both can hold deep feelings and beliefs about their roles and the impact that they can have in the organization. It is the deep down commitment that they share that makes them both engaged, and this is the kind of emotion that we are talking about here.

It doesn't matter if the emotions are displayed or not; it is what is felt inside that is important and that translates into increased performance. This is what a manager should be striving to obtain, and can only be achieved by making the connection between the employee, the employee's job, and the Vision of the organization. This is the role that managers must learn to excel at. It begins with Building Trust and Personal Responsibility; by respecting other's Personal Power.

Asking the Right Questions

Lesson 4

"Asking the right questions, instead of asking for the right answers, allow us to know the function rather than the effect of our choices."

Lesson 5

"Questioning our assumptions allows us to recognize underlying meanings or truths and the relative value of choices made."

LIFE LESSONS FROM THE RULE OF OPPOSITES

MICHAEL GARRETT

WALKING ON THE WIND

One of the best places to start in creating emotional connections is by asking questions. In his book *Winning*, Jack Welch commented that as an individual contributor you are expected to have the right answers to questions. When you become a manager you need to stop having the right answers and you need to start having the right questions. When managers stop telling people what to do and instead ask people questions so that employees can solve problems on their own, a manager begins to build Personal Responsibility in their employees. As employees answer the right questions and solve the right problems, they feel more committed to those solutions. They want the solution to be successful, and therefore commit more of their discretionary effort towards its success. This, of course, leads to the overall success of the organization.

Asking the right questions takes us back to *Intent*. This isn't something that just happens on its own. Managers must be cognizant of what is happening in the organization, in their workgroup, and in the external environment. A manager must carefully think about what questions need to be asked and to whom those questions need to be asked. They also need to think about how those questions need to be framed, keeping in mind that they will either be Building Trust or Destroying Trust if they are not careful.

In fact, it probably takes more energy and conscious effort to ask the right questions than it does to simply tell people what to do. As we have seen in Chapter 1, there is no comparison in the results. Managers who take the time and make the effort are rewarded with superior performance from their teams and for their organizations.

One of the best questions to ask is "why." But be careful how you ask it. If you ask "why" in a challenging way, others will become defensive. Instead, take the approach of a child. When we were children we often asked "why" about a lot of things. In fact, we often followed up an answer to our initial "why" question with a string of more "whys." Often they were asked in an inquisitive manner, and those "why" questions would probably have gotten answers that had been given more time and thought to their answers, as opposed to when we demanded an answer of "why" as part of throwing a tantrum to something we didn't want to do.

The same childlike, inquisitive approach can and should be taken by managers when asking questions. I believe that asking "why" and finding those answers help the organization to move forward, and also motivate people. Employees like to know why they are doing certain things in a certain way. The answer to "why" helps us to understand the importance of what we are doing and the constraints surrounding it. If the answer to "why" is a good answer, it can often allow people, employees, and customers alike, to accept situations that are less than desirable.

Continuing to ask "why" about a situation is also a good way to get to the bottom of a problem. When I was teaching Total Quality Management practices throughout the organization of one of my previous employers we often taught what was called "The 5 Whys." The technique calls for stating the problem and then asking "why." Once you answer that "why" you then ask "why" again, and then come up with the answer to that "why." You continue asking "why" and answering each "why" until you have asked and answered "why" at least five times. Doing this helps uncover the layers of issues that so often hide the real underlying issue that keeps us from making real progress in solving problems and being innovative.

I believe that more organizations should incorporate the word "why" into the language of their culture and make it a way of doing business. If they did, then it would no longer be a threat to others when asked, and we would actually get good answers when "why" is asked. This would result in a lot more problems being solved. Employees would also have a greater understanding of the reasons and importance of what they are doing.

Leadership Focus Depends on Level

The key to being a successful manager at any level is to always remember that your primary role is that of Leader, and the primary goal is to increase employee engagement. It doesn't matter what level of management a manager might be, the primary role and goal is always the same. However, where the focus is placed is different.

For executives and higher level managers, their focus for creating emotional connections is going to be more towards the East of the Medicine Wheel. Their primary function as a leader is to insure that the Vision of the organization, its Purpose, Values, and Goals, are carefully drafted and that they are communicated incessantly throughout the organization. They must also insure that everyone, beginning at their level on down, is living the Vision and that the organization's culture is fostering Trust and Personal Responsibility. This kind of focus provides the stability and importance that employees need in order to become emotionally engaged in the first place.

For lower level managers, their focus for creating emotional connections is going to be more towards the West of the Medicine Wheel (see Chapter 7). Their primary function as a leader is to work directly with the employee to insure that the employee understands how their particular job is important and is directly linked to the performance of the organization. This is the level where the Vision is lived, and where conversations about acceptable behaviors for Building Trust and Personal Responsibility must occur.

Sure, the operations of the organization are important, and that is what most managers in most organizations focus on. But managers in the best organizations realize that if they have clearly identified the Purpose, Values and Goals of the organization and carefully and constantly communicated them to everyone in the organization, then they can rely on their highly engaged and committed employees to look out for the operations of the organization. Managers in the best organizations realize that they must put their emphasis on building the foundation of the organization and then creating emotional connections in the employees to the organization and its Vision.

It is Leadership behavior, not Director behavior that supports and allows the other seven elements to work and create high performance in an organization.

CHAPTER 7

Focus on Strengths and Accentuate the Positive

The West is the direction of the Physical, and as I shared in Chapter 5, just as I wrestled a lot with what was going on in the East, this direction also gave me some trouble. Quite simply, I was unsure what lessons this direction was trying to teach. It wasn't until I came across a growing body of research by Gallup and a related body of research initially shared by David Cooperrider that it all came together. This body of research clearly supported the attributes of the West of the Medicine Wheel.

The research was becoming clearer to me; the best organizations focused at all levels on what they did well and not on what they didn't do well. In other words, they focused on their strengths and not on their weaknesses. This starts at the very top when crafting the organization's Vision. James Collins and Jerry Porras shared in *Built to Last* that the "visionary" and "great" companies, when identifying their core (Purpose and Values), focused on what they were the best at, not on what they were poor at doing and wanted to get better at doing. This was very evident with Collins' sharing of the Hedgehog Concept, where the "great" companies identified what they were passionate about; what they could make money at; and what they could be the best in the world at. Marcus Buckingham also shared in *The One Thing You Need to Know* about Gallup's research in the areas of Strengths research from the top of the organization right down to the individual contributor.

I found it rather fascinating that this East-West axis was the one that gave me such a problem, as this axis is the embodiment of Being versus Doing. If we find that the East defines what we are to Be, then the West helps us define how we are going to Do what needs to be done to achieve our Being. And just as I was having problems trying to understand this axis, most organizations have a hard time putting the concepts of this axis into action so that it makes a difference in their performance. If high performance organizations are different in how they identify and cling to the very core of their Being, then they are equally as different in how they go about day-to-day activities as they accomplish their Doing.

Positive verses Negative

One of the key components of utilizing Strengths is that when we look at situations and work with people we don't focus on what is going wrong, but rather we focus on what is going right. Now, this does not mean that we don't acknowledge problems or issues and the reality of situations. What it does mean is that instead of focusing on what happened that is going wrong, we focus on what is right and what we want to achieve.

This is akin to a lot of other theories, including what has been termed "The Law of Attraction." In other words, what you tend to focus on is what you tend to get. If we focus on what is going wrong, instead of getting more of what we want we tend to get more of what is wrong. Or, if we do happen to get less of what is wrong it doesn't always follow that we will get more of what is right or what we need in order to succeed. On the other hand, if we focus on what is right and work towards getting more of it, then as what is right happens more and more frequently we will see less and less of what is going wrong.

Accentuating the Positive also helps to engage people; employees and customers. While we have all come across those few rare people who seem to love to wallow in negativity, most people would prefer to be surrounded by the good feelings that come from being positive. Remember that engagement comes from the positive side of emotions, not the negative.

Using Strengths for Strategy

As I have previously shared, the beginning of a Vision is the understanding of the organization's Purpose; why it exists other than to make money. This is clearly a defining moment for any organization. If an organization carelessly chooses to pursue a Purpose that is not something that it can reasonably attain, then the likelihood that the organization will fail is high. As Collins shared in his hedgehog concept, the Purpose of an organization must come from what it is strong at doing.

The same thing applies to selecting the Goals that the organization will use to achieve its Purpose. Often in strategic planning and strategic goal setting, management will go through a common exercise called a SWOT Analysis. This is where the organization tries to identify its strengths, weaknesses, opportunities, and threats. But if we utilize the Strengths approach and Accentuate the Positive, then as we focus on our goals and set our initiatives, we would look only for our strengths and opportunities and accentuate those. Focusing on weaknesses and threats are only a waste of time.

Let me give an example of this. Several years ago my wife and I attended a motorcycle safety course. One of the things that they taught us was that to avoid a pothole that we needed to look where we wanted to go, not at the pothole. If we looked at the pothole then we would tend to end up bouncing through it because where we focused was where we tended to go. Thus, if we focused where we wanted to go, and not on where we didn't want to go, then we would get to where we wanted to go.

In other words, we need to indentify what we want to Be, first; then we need to identify what we want to Achieve by setting our Goals. Then we can focus on what we need to Do to Achieve our Goals. To do this we need to understand the organization's Strengths and how we can use those Strengths to Achieve our Goals. We also need to have a thorough understanding of the situation and the internal and external environments, which might impact our ability to leverage those Strengths.

On the other hand, we do not worry about our weaknesses, as the time and resources needed to overcome those would be a distraction from achieving our goals, just as a pothole is a distraction on the road. We also don't worry about threats, as they may or may not emerge. If they do emerge, then they are now a part of the environment and we would have identified them as part of the situation and we can bring our strengths to bear. Besides, a threat, by definition, may or may not actually appear. If a threat does actually become an obstacle then we only have a few options to deal with it; work through it or work around it to overcome it. Failing to overcome the obstacle is not an option, as that would mean not achieving a Goal.

By focusing on Strengths and Accentuating the Positive, the organization can now focus its resources on the key things that are going to make a difference in the performance of the organization, and not be wasting time, resources, and squandering emotional engagement on those things that simply distract from performance. This kind of focus is what allows high performing organizations to outperform their competitors.

Using Strengths for Employee Performance

As we discussed in Chapter 6, Leadership behavior is usually focused towards the East and Vision, or to the West and with helping employees with performance in their job. Utilizing Strengths is one of the tools for leaders to use in helping to create those emotional connections and drive employee performance. As I have shared earlier, it must begin with a clear organizational Vision. If employees are unsure of why the organization is important, then they won't understand why their job is important.

This same clarity transfers to the actual position that the employee is filling. There are four components to creating clarity and a connection between the employee's job and the Vision of the organization. These are: Purpose of the position; Roles that the employee will fill; Responsibilities for each of the roles; and Results that the employee will be expected to obtain.

Purpose: When creating a position the organization must identify why this position exists. Employees need to know why their position is important and how it helps the organization achieve its goals. There needs to be a clear link between the purpose of the position and the purpose of the organization.

Roles: Most positions have a number of roles that are involved in accomplishing its purpose, unless it is of the most menial type. Even a seemingly simple position, such as a stock clerk, can have a number of roles. It is important to identify each of these roles so that employees can be clear about what is involved in their job. Be careful; don't identify too many roles. Two to three would be average and four would be pushing the limit. Roles are not tasks, but the overall arching "hat" that the employee wears.

> *Role Prioritization* – Oftentimes there are numerous demands on an employee's time and focus. In order to reduce role conflict and having an employee focus on the wrong thing at the wrong time, Roles should be prioritized as to their importance, including any times where there might be an exception to that prioritization. In addition, employees should know the approximate percentage of their time would be spent on each Role. Just because a particular Role might have a high priority does not mean that a lot of time will be spent on it.

Responsibilities: Again, this is not about the tasks that the employee will perform, or what they will be "held accountable for." As we discussed in Chapter 4, Personal Responsibility is about being able to make decisions. We should be sharing with each employee what things that they are allowed to make decisions about regarding a given role. Remember that decisions made will always be in accordance with the organization's Values and in keeping with Building Trust and Personal Responsibility with others in the organization.

Results: This area concerns the objective measures that the employee will be responsible for achieving. These results must be cascaded down from the organization's Goals that are part of its Vision. Employees should have some way of tracking these objective measures in real time. Again, keep the number of measures to a minimum, usually three or less total across all roles.

Note that I've not mentioned anything about position descriptions or performance appraisals. In all of my research I did not find one mention where either of these things drove performance for the organization. We have got to stop focusing on individual performance measures and begin to focus more on group and organizational performance measures if we want to drive increases in organizational performance. As I have shared previously, any single person can perform greatly, but if others on the team or down the line aren't performing as well, then those great gains can end up meaning nothing to the performance of the organization. It is all the more reason why we must insure that performance measures (results) are directly linked back to and cascaded down from the team, department, division, and organizational goals.

It is far more important for employees to have a clear understanding of the Purpose, Roles, Responsibilities and real time Results for their position than it is to have a form filled out once a year telling them what someone believes their past performance has been. Performance appraisals only tell an employee about the past, not about their current performance and what they need to do to increase it for the future.

"The task of Leadership is to create an alignment of strengths in a way to make our weaknesses irrelevant."

PETER DRUCKER

This brings us to another function of being a Leader; that of performance coach. In Chapter 6 we learned about the importance of asking questions to find solutions. As a performance coach, the manager's role as a leader is to help employees discover their Strengths and to find a better way of doing things that works for them within the parameters of the processes and other organizational constraints. Any manager who has worked with people for very long will easily recognize that each employee has their own set of talents or Strengths. We need to cultivate their Strengths so that they can make the most of what they already have.

This means that managers should not be focusing on how things get done, but how well things get done. In speaking of Roles, Responsibilities, and Results, notice that I often said that the focus is not on tasks. Employees should be determining the tasks they need to perform, utilizing and playing off of their own individual Strengths, in order to achieve their results. Please note, however, this isn't an approach of "anything goes." We have to keep in mind that the employee can't Destroy Trust, which would involve the violation of ethics or laws, and they can't violate the Values of the organization. They would also have to stay within the processes that have been mapped by the organization (see Chapter 8 for more information on this).

By asking the right questions to find solutions, managers can help employees discover what their Strengths are and various ways to help develop and implement those Strengths in order to positively impact performance. Remember the focus should be on developing a person's Strengths rather than having a focus on "fixing" people. If you will recall the story I shared in Chapter 6 about the HR manager that wanted to "fix" her employee, an employee that really didn't need to be "fixed" at all. Too often the focus of development efforts is to put into people what Creator left out, rather than to develop the gifts that have already been given. Yet, this is exactly one of the attributes of the West; to develop the gifts that we already have.

Before we leave the West I would like to leave you with one final thought. When putting Strengths into action in the course of dealing with day-to-day performance, rely on the boundaries that Values and the Four Behaviors that Build Trust give us, and keep rules to a minimum. If you do have to rely on rules, then keep in mind what Vine Deloria, Jr., a prominent American Indian leader and philosopher of the mid to late 1900s once shared. He said that rules should tell us what we can achieve, not what we can't do. This approach keeps rules focused on the positive, and the achievement of Goals, rather than on the negative and what can't or shouldn't be done.

Don't believe that this won't work? I have a friend who works in the human resources department for a major technology company that has transformed their organization and as a result has accomplished phenomenal things. One of the first things they did in their transformation process was get rid of their HR policy and rule manual and rely on their Values to guide them in dealing with daily issues with employees. You see, Accentuating the Positive means that you have to do it in all things, not just a few. So, yes, you can try ditching your rules, or, at the very least, insure that what rules you do retain are focused on the positive and the achievement of your Goals.

When you have disciplined people, you don't need hierarchy. When you have disciplined thought, you don't need bureaucracy. When you have disciplined action, you don't need excessive controls.

JIM COLLINS
GOOD TO GREAT

CHAPTER 8

Encourage Innovation, because Good Enough is Not Enough

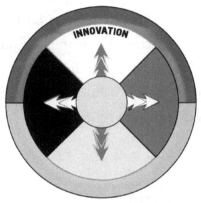

As we move from the West to the North we enter the realm of the Mental. This is a place for solving problems and the application of knowledge. It is a perfect place for the residence of our final element: Innovation. Much of the research indicated that the best organizations never stayed still. They were constantly trying to improve their organization, their products, their services, their relationships, and their internal operations. In their book, *Built to Last*, Collins and Porras share from their research a concept of "preserve the core and stimulate progress." In other words, the best organizations were crystal clear about who they were (their Purpose, Values and Goals), but at the same time they were also adapting to the ever-changing world around them to provide the best possible product or service to their customers.

Unfortunately, too many organizations have a mentality of mediocrity. They are happy with doing what they have to do to just get by. They get caught up in believing that because they have always done something the same way that it should be good enough. One of the reasons why many organizations aren't willing to move out of their mentality of mediocrity is that being innovative is tough and challenging. It takes a lot of resources; time, people, energy, focus, and, yes, money. But as we saw in Chapter 1, the returns are more than worth it. The difference between the best organizations and the rest is that the best organizations believe that good enough is never enough.

In reviewing the research there are a lot of different ways that the best organizations take towards creating a climate for Innovation. Each is optimized for that organization and is based on its unique circumstances, such as culture, industry, size, market, and so on. But there are four areas that seem to be in common for all, so let's explore those areas.

Controlling Processes

The first step in creating a climate of Innovation is to have a clear understanding of how an organization's operations function. If an organization has clearly identified its Goals, including initiatives, then the next step is to identify each of the processes that the organization will have to undertake to achieve those Goals. The organization then needs to identify each of its current processes, and then compare the two. This gives the organization an opportunity to determine which processes it needs to continue doing, start doing, or stop doing. Only those processes that are key to achieving the organization's goals need to remain.

The next step is to map those processes and bring them under control. Whether you call it TQM, Six Sigma, Business Process Reengineering, Lean Manufacturing, or some other term, the concept is the same; you are controlling your processes through the use of some form of structured discipline using some form of statistical measures and controls. I simply prefer to call the entire group Statistical Process Control (SPC). But whatever you call it, this is a critical part of Innovation. If you don't know what you are doing in your operations, then how can you improve them? If people aren't following some sort of process, then how can you insure that every customer is going to get your best?

While the manufacturing world has more readily adopted SPC, it is applicable to any organization in any industry. I personally have had success working with clients in government and social services, as well as in manufacturing. Unfortunately, our manufacturing industry is shrinking in the United States, while we see an ever-increasing expansion of organizations in the areas of service, social services and government agencies, and the organizations in these areas are probably the worst at mapping and controlling their processes. Every organization has processes and every organization should identify those processes and map them so that they can be controlled. Once a process is controlled you can then begin to work on it to make it better.

I'm not going to go into the steps of identifying, mapping, controlling, and improving processes in this book. There are way too many books available on the subject, and there are way too many methods to utilize. An organization must choose the method that works best for its culture and its circumstances. I do want to share one caution, however, in using any of the many methods out there; don't control your processes too tightly. Just as we don't want to control our People too tightly, we also don't want to overly control our processes too tightly, either.

By over controlling processes we reduce the variability of the processes, but at the expense of no longer allowing individuals to best utilize their unique Strengths. We end up making everyone operate the same, rather than allowing them to operate at their optimum ability. The key to achieving this balance between control of processes and leveraging the Strengths of your People is to map the process based on what you want to achieve at each step, not how it is achieved. Only in those rare circumstances where "how" is really important should we go into that kind of detail.

Once an organization's processes have been mapped and controlled the organization can now begin to work on making improvements to meet and exceed customer demands and expectations.

Change

The mystery of all ending is found in the birth and new beginnings.

THE SACRED TREE

Change is an integral part of Innovation. The Medicine Wheel teaches four key lessons regarding successful change. First, it teaches us that change must come from within, and that is what Innovation allows us to do; to take control of the change that is happening around us and drive our own change within our organization. All too often most organizations simply are reacting to the change that is happening around them. The best organizations are creating their own change from inside and driving progress forward despite what is happening around them.

The Medicine Wheel also teaches us that lasting change has to come from having a Vision. We can't make change work for us unless we have been clear about who we are and where we are going. Understanding our Purpose and Values creates the boundaries for any change, and understanding our Goals provides us with the direction for change. Otherwise, what often happens is that organizations experience an unending cycle of changes for change's sake, and not for the sake of achieving success for the organization.

Change must also come from having "a great insight." In other words, everyone must understand the change and the reasons for the change. Without this understanding, people most likely will not be committed to the change and its success. This is a key point, as Innovation lies in the North and the realm of the Mental, change is very much rooted in the South and the realm of the Emotional.

I once attended a training session by Dr. William Bridges, a renowned thought leader in the area of change management. He shared with us that change, in itself, is rather easy to craft. You design the changes and set a date; one day things are one way, the next day things are different. It isn't the change that is so difficult, but people's reaction to that change that is hard. It is this human side of change that most organizations fail to deal with effectively.

The key to dealing with the human side of change is, of course, Leadership and creating emotional connections. Leaders must insure that everyone understands the reason for the changes and how the changes will help the organization achieve its Goals and Purpose. Leaders must also communicate how these changes will specifically impact the individual and how these individual changes are going to be vital to the success of the organization. Everyone has their own concerns about how change will impact them. It is only by helping each employee to overcome their fears of the change and helping them to embrace the change that the change be accepted and end up being successful.

Finally, the Medicine Wheel teaches us that there must be "a healing forest present" in order for the change to survive. This means that there must be the support and resources available for the change to be effectively implemented. It also means that others need to be made aware of the change, even if they aren't directly involved. This allows those who might come in contact with those who have been impacted by the change will not unintentionally undermine the change. It also allows others to provide emotional support and encouragement throughout the change.

This may mean that other departments that interact on a regular basis might be made aware of a recent change in another department, or it might mean that the organization shares changes with their customers. Either way, sharing about the change allows for healing to occur as people leave behind the old ways, and it also allows for commitment to the new ways. Do not doubt that there will be grieving over leaving the old ways behind. This is why it is so crucial for organizations to clearly communicate the insights regarding the change and provide the support for implementing if change is going to be successful.

The Four Laws of Successful Change

1. Change comes from within

2. Permanent change requires a Vision

3. A great insight must occur

4. A healing forest must be present

The Innovation Process

That's right; Innovation is not something that just happens haphazardly. It is the result of a process that begins with creativity and ends with execution. Creativity (idea generation) alone is not Innovation; newly generated ideas have to be put into action before there is Innovation.

Innovation is about action and moving forward, not just generating ideas. When Jim Collins talks about "stimulating progress" this is what he is talking about. Simply generating ideas and not taking action will not stimulate progress.

Only when the new ideas are put into action will we know if the Innovation has an impact on the performance of the organization. Otherwise, if we are spending money on generating new ideas, advancing them and refining them but never implement them, then we can never gain a return and it can only cost the organization.

One of the things that I like about this approach is that not everyone has to feel like they have to be "creative" (whatever that seems to mean) to be able to contribute to helping the organization be Innovative. While not everyone is "creative," usually most have ideas, and that is what we need to be encouraging: the sharing of ideas. If we allow people to utilize their natural talents to help out in the Innovation process, then they will be far more engaged and feel as if they can contribute.

So just what is the Innovation process? In his book *Innovation on Demand*, Al Fahden shares a four-stage process for Innovation:

Creating Stage – Ideas for finding and solving problems are generated. There is no value placed on any of the ideas. The goal is to generate as many ideas as possible, not to judge them.

Advancing Stage – Ideas are reviewed and chosen based on their potential ability of being successful at solving the problem. Some ideas might be good, but may not be possible to be implemented. Others might take more resources than are practical. Out of many ideas usually only a few are practical, and those are the ones that should be advanced.

Refining Stage – Ideas chosen to move forward are refined so that they have a better chance of actually solving the problem. Implementation issues are also addressed.

Execution Stage – A plan for implementation of the final solution is developed and the idea is actually executed. Success of execution is monitored.

Please take note that this process is not linear. Ideas might be created and advanced to the point where they are being refined and another problem is discovered. In order to solve that problem we would then go back to the creating stage and begin again, working on that particular issue. We may undergo several rounds of this before we finally end up with a fully refined idea that can be successfully executed.

Let me give you an example of how this process might work:

Several team members are working on a project to solve a problem. Member C is in a room thinking about the problem and starts writing ideas that may or may not work on a white board, just tossing out a bunch of ideas.

Member A walks in and looks over the board and says, "Hey, wait a minute! The next to the last idea is intriguing. I think that might be a solution."

Member R is walking by and hears this and walks in the room and looks at the idea that A was talking about. "Well, this is pretty rough and it will need some work, but let me see what adjustments we can make to see if we can make it work." R sits down and starts jotting down some notes and goes off to work on refining the idea. In the meantime Member E is told by A that they might have a solution and that R is working on trying to polish some things. Member E stops by to see R and to see how things are coming along.

Member E says to R, "I don't know if we can get this implemented this way. There is a problem with this component being able to integrate with the fluglebinder on the biggleworts. This is close, but we need to see if we can fix the integration issue." R and E then go back to C and A to start again, this time C is generating ideas to make sure they can integrate with the fluglebinder.

Another way to explain this is through the thinking styles of each person that naturally fits each step in the innovation process, as it does take different ways of thinking to be innovative:

Creator - combination of spontaneous and conceptual thinking styles; focuses on the possibilities; generates ideas

Advancer - combination of spontaneous and normative thinking styles; focuses on the interactions; promotes ideas

Refiner - combination of methodical and conceptual thinking styles; focuses on analysis; challenges ideas

Executor - combination of methodical and normative thinking styles; focuses on realities; implements ideas

Here is another example – according to a thinking styles profile, I am a Creator-Refiner and my wife, my partner in my business and who runs the behind the scenes stuff, is an Advancer. I have a horrible habit of coming up with ideas, trying to polish them, and then coming up with another idea and polishing that one. Unfortunately I waste a lot of time getting stuck in the creating/refining cycle and all too frequently nothing moves forward and gets executed.

When I do ask my wife what she thinks she will sometimes tell me that an idea is a waste of time. Sometimes I ignore her and refine it anyway, and then try to implement it. Most of the time it fails and she says, "I told you not to do that."

By understanding the Innovation process model I have learned two things. First, before I go off refining an idea I need to run it by my wife to see what she thinks. When she is negative about an idea I now ask her what her concerns are and then go off to try to come up with new ideas around her answer. Second, I have learned that neither of us are executors, and that we can get distracted by my tendency to generate new ideas and not follow through with ideas that have been refined and are waiting to be put into action. We both have to force ourselves to play the role of Executor and think about things from that point of view. Sometimes it is very hard, but it can be done, and must be done if we are going to be successful in our business.

Mastering this process of idea generation to idea implementation is precisely what the best organizations have done. Just because Innovation is the last element of the Seven Elements of High Performance does not mean that it is the least important. I believe that the other elements must be in place for consistent Innovation to make an impact on the performance of the organization. I also believe that if an organization will provide the other six elements that it can't help but experience Innovation, because their engaged employees will not let the organization not take advantage of opportunities to be Innovative and Achieve its Goals, and ultimately, its Purpose.

Diversity

All the races and tribes in the world are like the different colored flowers of the meadow. All are beautiful. As children of our Creator they must be respected.

FROM *THE SACRED TREE*

For over two decades, diversity has been a hot topic in many organizations. Unfortunately, most organizations still seem to struggle with the concept and how it can make a difference in their organization. If we understand that the power for an organization to be both successful and significant lies in its People, then we can begin to get a glimpse of how diversity can impact Innovation. For the Innovation process to be successful, it is imperative that we have a wealth of ideas at each stage in the process. This means that we need to have people from a variety of backgrounds and experiences so that they can look at the situation from a number of different perspectives.

One of the things that the Medicine Wheel teaches us is that everything exists in a Circle, where there is no beginning and no end. Truth lies somewhere within this Circle, its exact location depending upon where in the Circle a person stands. Instead of opposites lying at the end of a straight-line continuum, they lie on opposite sides of the Circle. This creates a blending of the opposites, for where one ends the other begins.

The more perspectives we can have of the Truth within the Circle, the more likely it is that we will be able to find solutions that will make an impact on the performance of the organization. If we have too many employees who are too much alike, then they will tend to be clustered together in one part of the Circle, and will see but only one way of doing things. On the other hand, if we have a diversity of People, then we will have employees scattered all across the Circle with many different viewpoints. This gives us a better picture of the Truth, and a different perspective from which to generate ideas.

But this only happens when we accept others for who they are and the value that they bring to the table. Acceptance is one of the Four Behaviors that Build Trust, and it is vital not only to Building

Trust, but to the success of Innovation, as well. The main reason why diversity efforts have failed in the past is precisely because of this issue of Acceptance. Diversity efforts, including training, too often tend to be focused on "appreciating differences" in others, be it their sex, race, culture, or some other artificial barrier that we have created. What is needed is for People, no matter what their "difference," to be able to feel as if they can contribute to the success of the organization. When we accept people for who they are and what they can contribute then they feel included, and this inclusion leads to engagement and ownership, and...well, we know the rest. Simply put, any organization must have a diverse group of employees and engage those employees if it wants to make the most of the Innovation Process and achieve its Vision.

> *The individual is the fountainhead of creativity and innovation, and we are struggling to get all of our people to accept the countercultural truth that often the best way to manage people is just to get out of their way. Only by releasing the energy and fire of our employees can we achieve the decisive, continuous productivity advantages that will give us the freedom to compete and win in any business anywhere on the globe.*
>
> JACK WELCH
> *WINNING*

Diversity is about inclusion; inclusion leads to engagement; engagement leads to performance; performance leads to the achievement of the organization's Goals.

Coming Full Circle

CHAPTER 9

Be – Do – Achieve

When you compare great companies to good ones, many widely practiced business norms turn out to correlate with mediocrity, not greatness.

JIM COLLINS

GOOD TO GREAT AND THE SOCIAL SECTORS

Since I started conducting my research several of the books that I have referenced have become quite prominent and widely discussed in business circles. Jim Collins, Jack Welch, and Marcus Buckingham have become sought out speakers for all sorts of events. I have a friend who was very fortunate to be able to have lunch with Marcus before one such event. He shared with my friend that despite all of the research and sharing of information from that research, that very few organizations have actually changed how they operate and have focused on those things that really make a difference.

Instead of doing things differently, most organizations just talk differently, but keep doing the same things, all the while expecting to achieve the results that have been talked about in the research. In many organizations they are now doing "performance management." What this usually means is that they are still using their same performance appraisal system with some added technology component to track the administration, completion, and filing of the annual form. Their focus is still on rating an employee on some subjective measure that may or may not positively impact the organization's performance.

But relabeling isn't the worst. In most cases the focus is on still doing the same old practices that just about every organization does. What does it get them? The same results that everyone else is getting, which is average, mediocre performance. Most people just cannot understand that in order to take advantage of the research on high performance organizations, then you first have to want an organization that rises above the average to be one of the best and then you simply have to do things differently than what everyone else is doing.

A couple of years ago, as a sponsor for Small Business Month for the Gainesville, Florida Chamber of Commerce, I had the opportunity to serve on a number of panels with other experts and successful business owners. At these events I had the opportunity to meet a business owner whose company was extremely successful. I listened to him talk about how this wasn't always the case and that things didn't change until after he read the book Good to Great, and how that impacted his thinking.

He shared that he decided that they were going to make some changes in how his company operated. The first thing he did was take his management staff off on a two-day retreat, so that they could focus on determining their Purpose, Values, and Goals. He shared that six months later they were still trying to work on them. He said that it wasn't as easy as he thought it would be to identify what was important for driving the success of his business. It took them over nine months to finalize just their Purpose and Values.

Eventually, they were successful in indentifying the important things that were the core of the business. Then they started working on making sure that everything that they did fit with the Purpose, Values, and Goals that they had identified. This meant a lot of changes in how they operated, beginning with how they hired people, and ended with how they treated people with dignity and respect, even when once in a while employees didn't work out and they had to let them got.

He made sure that new employees were selected to fit the culture that he was building. He rewarded his best employees, and constantly kept all employees focused on what was important, not allowing employees to be sidetracked into doing things just because they had always done them. Everyone made sure that the actions they were taking always drove the organization forward, and everyone knew which direction forward was.

The result is that his business is now one of the most successful businesses in the area.

The research is very clear; there is a demarcation between what most organizations focus on and do and what the best organizations focus on and do. Most organizations just focus on doing things because they either believe that it is what is supposed to be done or because it has always been done that way. The best organizations first understand who they are and what they want to accomplish. Once they understand what they want to achieve, they then determine what they need to do to achieve it.

The signature of mediocrity is not an unwillingness to change; both the great and the non-great change a lot. The difference is that the great are always consistent with their values. The signature of mediocrity is not an unwillingness to change; the signature of mediocrity is chronic inconsistency.

JIM COLLINS
FROM A SPEECH AT FORTUNE 500 EVENT, 19 JAN 2009

In other words, most organizations simply do things that they hope will give them some sort of results that will help them be successful without defining what that success really looks like or knowing if the actions they are engaging in will help them be successful. They simply Do first, and then look to see what happened. The best organizations, on the other hand, have a deep understanding of who they are and what they want to achieve. They have a clear sense of Being. From this clear sense of Being they can then make decisions about what they need to Do to Achieve their Goals.

Be – Do – Achieve

This process allows the high performing organizations to tightly focus their resources on doing the things that will actually bring results to the organization, while eliminating those activities that do not provide value. As Jim Collins correctly stated, most of what most organizations do just doesn't add value to achieving results. So if you focus on doing what most organizations are doing, you will get what most organizations are getting, and most organizations are simply achieving mediocre results, at best.

The best organizations don't just do things differently; they do different things

Changing Perspectives

In order to be able to identify the new and different things that we need to be doing to increase the performance in our organization, we often have to change our location within the Circle so that we can find a new perspective. As we gain a new perspective, then we see things differently and can find new ways of doing different things, as opposed to doing the same things in just a different way.

One of the first perspectives that we need to change is regarding our beliefs about people. As I shared in Chapter 6 regarding Leadership, we must believe that we can trust the people that we hire. It also means that we must do things in our organizations that will insure that we continue to Build Trust with our employees and that when employees do things that Destroy Trust that they are removed. Of course, we have already talked about this in previous chapters.

This isn't the only area in which we must change our beliefs about People. In most organizations just about everything that they do is focused on getting rid of their employees. Whether it is an ad in the newspaper for a job opening, the application process, or interviews, the focus is on weeding out the least desirable. Once an employee is hired they may or may not receive some sort of orientation. They show up, maybe they are given some HR rules and they fill out a whole lot of HR paperwork. Then they are sent off to their workplace, which often isn't prepared for them. All too frequently people finally end up in their workplace with little welcome and even less attention.

In most organizations, new employees are usually placed on probation. This is a time where the organization makes a decision if they will retain the employee or not. If the employee makes it through probation then they are given an appraisal once a year where they learn if they have been good or not, and if they haven't, they are given an "improvement plan," which, if they fail to successfully meet, will lead to their dismissal.

Every step along the way, from the moment it is decided to hire someone, the organization is planning on how to have that person leave the organization. This kind of focus does nothing for making the employee feel trusted or valued, and it certainly doesn't do anything to engage the employee.

Contrast this focus with that of one of the best performing organizations. Their focus is on finding and retaining the best employees that they can find. Their hiring process is much longer, focusing on not just insuring that employees have the critical skills that the organization needs, but that the potential employees also fit with the culture of the organization.

Once employees are hired they aren't just sent to a half-day orientation to fill out forms and then off to be ignored in the workplace. They participate in a longer-termed on-boarding process that helps to integrate them into the organization. They learn about the organization's history, culture, Purpose, Values and Goals. They learn about how what they do fits into the greater picture of what the organization does.

Instead of being ignored when arriving in the workplace, their manager and coworkers are waiting to welcome the new employee.

Everyone, not just the training department or the manager, is responsible for insuring that the new employee knows what his or her job and team is all about. Instead of waiting for a once-a-year meeting and form, the new employee is given a set of measures that they are responsible for and can monitor on their own on a regular basis. Their manager is there to coach them to find new ways for improving their individual and their team's performance. They share with coworkers their ideas and provide feedback to each other.

If, for some reason, the employee is not performing well, then processes and tasks are reviewed and strengths are looked at to see where the problem might be. The assumption is not that the employee is lazy or obstinate, but rather that the tasks and the employee are not a good fit. If the employee's strengths aren't such that the employee can perform well in their current duties, then new duties are found that might be a better fit for them. After all, it is a lot harder to find someone who is a fit to the culture and is committed to the organization than it is to find new things for the employee to do that they can do well.

The best organizations believe that they have invested so much in hiring the best employees, not just in skills, but also the best fit with the organization's culture that all efforts are exhausted before the organization will make that decision to fire an employee. The only exception to this hesitation is when an employee does something to Destroy Trust or by violating the organization's Values, which is just another way to Destroy Trust.

By changing our perspectives about people we now begin to see how to do different things that will engage those people, and engaged people will now help us find even more "different things" to be doing in the organization that will help drive Innovation, take care of customers, and, ultimately, drive the performance of the organization.

New Perspectives and Rules

In Chapter 7, I talked about changing our perspective about rules. I shared that rules should tell us what we can achieve, not what we can't do. Yet, so often that is exactly what we get in most organizations. I recall that when I worked for a division of a governmental agency that we had a policy and procedure manual for the division that filled two three-inch three-ring binders. We also had organizational rules and regulations, and then we had the legal statues, which filled four volumes. How could anyone know what was in all of those books and insure that they followed everything?

It doesn't have to be this way. We can reduce rules and regulations, policies and procedures down to a minimum, with a focus on helping people to achieve their and their organization's goals. We can keep rules focused on the positive, and we can do it without jeopardizing the security of the organization. The reason we can do this is that we are now approaching people from our new and different perspective.

Usually when I start talking about the issue of limiting rules I often hear about how we are exposing the organization to all sorts of legal issues. I disagree. When employees sue their employer, it is because they feel that the organization has done something wrong to them. They feel disenfranchised and they feel that the organization does not care. Most lawsuits by employees surround the issues of firings, harassment, and pay. In other words, they are precisely about the kinds of disagreements that we can eliminate through our relationships we are building and through the Values and Trust that we have set as our guidelines for our behavior.

When we hire employees that we Trust, respect, and value, then they feel engaged. They will perform, especially when they know that performance problems will be dealt with fairly and with the end result focused on helping the employee to be better, not on punishment. When we value employees and teach them to value each other, we don't tend to have harassment problems. If someone does harass another employee, then that employee has Destroyed Trust, and they cannot stay, therefore, eliminating an environment where harassment can continue and be hostile. After all, engaged employees who are harassed don't want to sue the company, they simply want the harasser to stop.

When we value employees and are concerned with insuring their engagement, with a focus on performance, then we are not going to be involved in schemes that will short an employee's pay. We will pay our employees better than average, and when they help the organization perform well, we will share the results of that success with our employees.

Finally, if we do have to fire an employee for poor performance, it is much easier. When we track performance with objective measures, then we do not need to rely on subjective performance appraisal forms to demonstrate that poor performance. We can easily demonstrate the performance, we can show coaching meetings from the managers' logs, and we can demonstrate other actions that were taken to help the employee perform better, including the possible elimination of some tasks and the changing of others.

In the end, most employees that have been given the opportunity to improve in a supportive environment will eventually leave on their own, and not cause any kind of problems. If they do, the organization will have a much stronger position to defend.

What Works for You

Awhile back I was working with a client to help a group of their top managers to prepare for the Certified Manager exam that is offered by the Institute of Certified Professional Managers. This was an exciting and diverse group, with a variety of experience levels, and they were a joy to work with. They challenged me and kept me on my toes as I worked with them to not just prepare for their upcoming exam, but to also make a difference in the performance of their organization.

One day we were reviewing some case studies on what some of the best organizations did in regard to their people policies. We had just finished reviewing information about SAS Institute in Cary, North Carolina, and how they didn't have a sick leave policy. One of the younger managers asked a very innocent, yet insightful question. "If the best organizations are doing these things, then why don't we just do these things so that we can be the best?"

It was a very good question, and is an approach that many organizations try to follow, but with very few real results. As we explored the question, he soon came to realize that the decision that SAS Institute made on sick leave came out of the kind of work that their organization did and the kinds of work that people did in their organization. It was a result of their culture and Values, along with the Purpose and Goals they were trying to achieve. They then looked back over some of the other organizations and the approaches that they took to engage their People, and they found the same thing. Each organization's approach was based on the uniqueness of that particular organization, comprised of its industry, culture, Purpose, Values, and Goals.

The group of managers discovered from these case studies that while each organization placed an extreme emphasis on the value of its People, they approached demonstrating that value through its own unique culture. The managers then began talking about what their company's culture was all about and the kinds of things that they should consider in developing their own way of demonstrating the value of People in their organization.

The Seven Elements of High Performance are universal. They do not change from organization to organization, no matter what the industry is or what the culture is. What is different is in how these seven elements are applied in the organization. It is up to us to find the best way to put these seven elements to work; a way that fits within the high performance culture that we are trying to achieve; a way that works uniquely for us.

Communication Is the Key

When I was doing the Small Business Month sessions for the Chamber in Gainesville, I served on a panel that was discussing these kinds of "people issues" using an audience Q&A approach. At the end I was asked that if I could sum things up, what would be the one thing that I could recommend to managers that would have the greatest impact. I didn't hesitate one moment – communication.

If People are at the center of everything we do, and we are going to operate by Building Trust, Personal Responsibility and Values, then we must communicate about these ideas and the behaviors that support them. Simply put, Trust must have open and straightforward communication in order to thrive.

If we are going to make a connection between employees and the Purpose and Goals of the organization, then we must communicate about why the Purpose is important and how the Goals will help the organization achieve its Purpose.

If we are going to work with employees' Strengths and coach them to perform better, then we have to communicate with them about that. And if we are going to foster Innovation then everyone must communicate and contribute their ideas.

If we don't effectively communicate about the Seven Elements and what they mean to the success of the organization, then we are just not going to be successful. If we aren't clear about how we are going to apply the Seven Elements, then we are not going to be successful. If we are not willing to communicate, then we are not going to build the relationships that are going to give the organization that edge over its competition.

If an organization is looking for one thing to invest in for the development of its managers and employees, then there is no doubt in my mind; it is communication. Teaching everyone this important interpersonal skill is the key to unlocking the Seven Elements of High Performance.

Be – Do – Achieve

- To **Achieve** what you have never had, you must **Do** what you have never done.

- If you do what everyone else is doing, you will get what everyone else is getting.

- Most get *mediocrity*, at best.

- To **Achieve** what you have never had, you must **Do** what you have never done.

- To **Do** what you have never done, you must **Be** what you have never been.

Know what you need to **Be** first.

Then you will know what to **Do** to Achieve your **Goals!**

CHAPTER 10

The Circle Is Never Ending

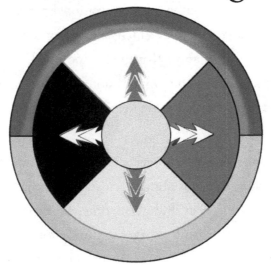

Should a person abandon the journey because they feel they have found all that they need in the gifts of one of the directions, great harm can come to them. For they will have shut themselves off from a large portion of their own true self, as well as created an imbalance that could bring harm.

THE SACRED TREE

I t seems that when we hear about growth in today's business world, we are talking about the organization becoming bigger or making more money. Rarely are we talking about the organization becoming better. There are a lot of organizations out there that have become bigger and made more money just before they fell apart, some of them even ceasing to exist. What the Medicine

Wheel teaches us is that while we must continually be growing, we can't rely on growth in any one area. We must grow across all areas if we are to thrive and survive.

As we begin working on applying the Seven Elements of High Performance to our organizations, we must learn that any one of the Seven Elements will not enhance organizational performance on their own. It takes all seven of the elements, working together in balance, to achieve high performance. If we place too much emphasis on any one of the elements then the organization can become out of balance and the Seven Elements can cease helping the organization achieve an advantage.

We must remember, however, that balance is not about equality. If you will recall, balance is about focusing efforts in those areas that most demand attention at any given time. So in the early stages of developing a high performing organization, efforts might be placed on developing Trust and a Vision. Later efforts might be placed on developing Leadership and Personal Responsibility, while later efforts might be placed on developing Strengths and Innovation.

We have to keep in mind that once we have developed one of the Seven Elements we are not finished with that element. As we develop other elements we will have to visit and revisit other elements. As I shared in Chapter 7, as we develop our Vision we will want to look to the West and our Strengths in order to discover and align our Purpose, Values, and Goals. As we develop Leadership we will want to visit both the East and the West in order to help create the emotional connections in our employees.

In other words, as we grow in each of the Seven Elements we must use the other Seven Elements for that growth. And as we continue to grow in any one of the Seven Elements, it helps us to grow in the other elements we are using. It is this continuous cycle that allows our organization to grow and perform. This growth should be continuous in all areas, and is represented by the arrows radiating from the center of the circle.

Sustainability

When we chose to dwell in any one of the Seven Elements, we do so at the detriment of the others. It is all too easy to become fixated on one particular solution to our problems and not realize that we have other resources available, or that, in fact, other resources are needed in order to fully solve our problems. This kind of focus on growth in any one area jeopardizes the survivability of the organization. The goal of the organization should never be solely on growth, but rather on growth and balance. Together, growth and balance bring about sustainability.

The focus then shifts from simply growing the organization to that of insuring the sustainability of the organization. We cannot make decisions about our organization today that will give us short-term results for tomorrow, but that place the organization's survival in peril for the future. When we understand that our organization can only survive within the context of our environment and can only thrive through the leveraging of the Seven Elements, we then can make better decisions that will impact the future of the organization. After all, the goal of the organization is not simply to perform, but to consistently perform and survive.

One of the lessons from the Medicine Wheel can help us with making good decisions to help insure the sustainability of our organization. The Medicine Wheel teaches us that we should make decisions based on the impact of that decision not for just today or tomorrow, but on the impact that decision will have on the seven generations to come. In other words, when we make our decisions we need to first compare them to our Values. Do the decisions that we have available support our Values? If not, then those that don't are discarded. Then we need to look at the long-term impact that the decision will have. Will it support and encourage the sustainability of our organization for seven generations? If not, then that decision should also be discarded.

> *A good example of what happens when we don't insure sustainability is from a local peanut processing company that is about 50 miles from us. This company has been in the news lately, but not for good things. From news reports we are learning that there were some serious violations of sanitary practices that resulted in the contamination of their processed peanut products, including peanut butter. The stories that we are hearing is that many employees reported and complained about the problems, but that management chose to overlook these issues and pushed for an increase in output of product. The focus was on trying to cut costs and increase revenues in some misguided attempt to drive profits.*

> *The result is that over 677 people across the country became sick and several died. There was a massive recall of products from the company, costing the processing company and those who it supplied huge amounts of dollars. The plant was shut down for inspection and it will never reopen. As a result of the plant closings, the company has filed for bankruptcy and is in the process of liquidation. Close to 100 people are now out of work and the owner and other top managers may be facing criminal charges.*

It is all too often that we are tempted to take the easy path of the short-term gains. If those gains will hurt the organization in the long-term then we are better off finding other paths. It becomes so much easier to take those paths and make those "harder" decisions when we keep the sustainability of the organization in mind. After all, as leaders and members of our organization, we have a responsibility to those who will become the leaders and members of the organization in the future.

Shattered Myths

Myth 3: Most successful companies exist first and foremost to maximize profits

Reality: Maximizing shareholder wealth has not been the dominant driving force through the history of visionary companies. Yet, paradoxically, they make more money than the purely profit-driven comparison companies

JIM COLLINS AND JERRY PORRAS
BUILT TO LAST

Jim Collins and Jerry Porras shared in *Built to Last* that the leaders of the best companies focused not on what they could accomplish for just now, but what they could build out of the company for the future. In his follow-up research shared in *Good to Great*, Jim Collins found similar results. The leadership of the "great" companies was not focused on their personal gain, but on the long-term success of their organization. In this book, I have often talked about how important having engaged employees is to the success of the organization. Engaged employees engage customers, and that drives performance. The leadership of the organization is totally responsible for insuring the sustainability of the organization.

Making the Most of the Circle

There are some key characteristics of the circle that can help a leader to create and sustain a high performance organization. These characteristics are:

The Circle has no beginning and no end.

The Circle is all-inclusive.

The Circle never stops turning.

The Circle turns best when it is balanced.

The same is true when applying the Seven Elements of High Performance to your organization. Work on developing your organization and maintaining its performance is never-ending. If you stop, the organization will deteriorate and performance will drop off. You must be ever vigilant in working with and applying the Seven Elements to your organization. You must use each of the Seven Elements together. They do not work separately and they do not work with just a few. You must use them all, and continue to learn and grow about how to use them better. You must also include everyone in your organization in the implementation of the elements in your organization. Keep focused on the long-term and do not allow easy gains to side-track or derail you from achieving your goals. And remember that what works best for your organization is based on its uniqueness and where it is located in the circle.

Any organization, for profit, non-profit, or government agency, has the opportunity to take advantage of the lessons from the Medicine Wheel. As we have discovered, the rewards can be very great. These rewards are not just in the performance of the organization as it achieves its goals. It is also an increase in the quality of life for all that are involved. Employees feel valued; leaders have fewer hassles;

customers have fewer frustrations. In the end, everyone enjoys life so much more. After all, life is just too short not to enjoy it, and there is no reason why the workplace can't be an enjoyable place to be for everyone.

All it takes for you and your organization to take advantage of these lessons from the Medicine Wheel is to:

- Put **People** at the *Center* of everything you do; employees, customers, and community

- Build **Trust** as a *Foundation*

- Allow **Personal Responsibility** through *Individual Decision Making*

- Share a **Vision** of an *Aligned Purpose, Values, and Goals*

- *Create Emotional Connections* through **Leadership**

- Focus on **Strengths** and *Accentuate the Positive*

- Encourage **Innovation**, because *Good Enough is Not Enough*

THE MEDICINE WHEEL TURNS FOREVER!

Epilogue

Thank you for allowing me to share with you the results of my personal and professional journeys. The insights that I achieved from my learning come almost by accident, yet also because I was open to the possibilities of what might be revealed. It seems that some of the most profound life lessons come when we least expect them and when we are most open to receive.

As I reviewed all of the research and reflected on my own workplace experiences, one of my greatest insights is that too often people are just not excited about their jobs. There are too many people who go to work every day dreading the day and what awaits them until the time they reach home again. Too many employees put up with the week just to reach their weekend. What ends up happening is that we end up wishing our life away, living for those few moments that give us pleasure or escape from the monotony of work. It just doesn't have to be that way, nor should it be. Unfortunately, the workplaces that too many managers create are usually the culprits for zapping that excitement from the spirits of their employees. But managers who want to make a difference can. Organizations can provide a focused, disciplined, exciting, and, yes, even fun place to work, while at the same time achieving its goals.

One of the things I've often thought is that there should be no reason why people should not want to go to work and spend time there achieving great things that they are highly interested in, just as much as they look forward to the weekend. There are some organizations out there that do understand this. Their employees love to go to work because they understand that they are making a difference. I just can't imagine why any business owner, CEO, or manager wouldn't want to have this kind of work environment for their employees and the organizational results that go with it. I would think that there would be great peace of mind that would come from having fewer hassles throughout the workday.

My hope is that what I have shared from my journey will help others to find a way to bring about the energy and focus necessary to create that great workplace in their own organization. It so often seems like a daunting task to make the changes necessary to energize employees and drive organizational performance. While still complex, I hope that the lessons from the Medicine Wheel will help leaders to find the ways to put the Seven Elements of High Performance into action for their organization.

I would like to share with you one final lesson from the Medicine Wheel. One of the things that the Medicine Wheel teaches us is that when offered gifts from others that we should take what we need and then blow the rest away with a breath of kindness. We should not refuse them with scorn because we have no immediate need. I realize that a lot of what I have shared challenges conventional business practices. But keep in mind that what I have shared not only has its foundation in ageless philosophy, but it is also supported by a wealth of research.

Perhaps you remain skeptical; that is okay. In traditional American Indian fashion, it is really for you to decide what learning you have need of at this time and what you will walk away with after reading this book. Perhaps later on, as you continue to think about what I have shared, and maybe even try some things, you might find new meanings and new value from these lessons.

In the meantime, my journey of learning also continues. Since starting this book, Ann and I have relocated our home and business from Lake City, Florida to Macon, Georgia. Due to circumstances beyond our control, the move actually took us just over a year to complete. This also delayed the completion of this book by a year, which I wished could have been avoided, but was just the reality of the situation.

Of course, this move also left us a very long ways from our favorite restaurant with Kyle and his staff. As things would turn out, Kyle also moved and ended up as a manager of an *On the Border* restaurant in Atlanta, which is actually the closest *On the Border* restaurant to our new home. Now, instead of driving 47 miles one way, we drive 87 miles one way to visit him and his new staff. We are looking forward to building relationships with a whole new group of people there. We might not be able to go to our favorite place as often as we once did, but Kyle can still count on us to pay him a visit on a regular basis. We are definitely engaged customers.

Also, since my discovery of the Seven Elements I am constantly trying to understand the relationships and intricacies between and among those elements. Clearly there are some strong relationships between Vision and Strengths, Leadership and Innovation, and Trust and Personal Responsibility. Supporting and contrasting, each of these elements exists in that symbiotic relationship that seems to lend an enhanced power to them because of their combinations. It isn't enough to realize that the relationships exist. It is more important to be able to apply those relationships in a way that can help people use them and the Seven Elements to help them and their organizations become more successful.

As a result, in addition to my own continued study of the Seven Elements, I am working on developing tools, exercises, activities, and programs that will help business owners and executives create a compelling Vision for their organization, and managers to learn how to create emotional connections and engage their employees. Of course, everything is all based on and designed to make the most of the Seven Elements. As I continue my work with clients, I continue to learn just as much as they do.

As I continue to work more with the Seven Elements of High Performance, in action and application, and as I continue to learn, my plans are to continue to share that learning with you in future articles and books. I welcome your comments and especially the sharing of your experiences as you walk your own journey in applying the Seven Elements of High Performance.

I very much look forward to sharing more with you in the future. Again, thank you for allowing me to share my journey with you.

Wado (Thank You)

For more information and resources, join us at www.LeadershipLessonsFromTheMedicineWheel.com, where you can also share your thoughts, ideas, and successes using the Seven Elements of High Performance™.

Future Books Based on
The Seven Elements of High Performance™

In Quest of a Vision: Creating High Performance Strategy

*Leadership Connections: Engaging
Employees for High Performance*

*The Seven Elements of High Performance™
in Action: Case Studies for Success*

*Life Lessons from the Medicine Wheel: The
Seven Elements for Personal Success™*

About Gary Lear

International speaker, trainer, researcher, and award-winning consultant, Gary Lear is the President & CEO of **Resource Development Systems** LLC, an organizational performance consulting firm that helps organizations increase performance by helping them to be successful at *Managing the Human Side of Business*sm.

Since starting **Resource Development Systems** LLC in 1997, Gary has worked with a variety of government, non-profit, and for profit organizations, including developing culturally sensitive programs for the US Department of Justice, and providing leadership development for such organizations as the US Army, Wal-Mart, and the Abu Dhabi National Oil Company in the United Arab Emirates. His **Seven Elements of High Performance**™ model for organizational performance has been chosen by the US Navy's Center for Naval Leadership to be included in their officer leadership curriculum.

Gary earned his bachelor's in psychology at Stetson University and did his master's work at the University of Central Florida in industrial/organizational psychology. Gary has served as an adjunct instructor at Daytona Beach and Lake City Community Colleges in Florida, and is currently an adjunct instructor for Central Georgia Technical College in Macon, Georgia, the National Institute of Corrections in Aurora, Colorado and the Institute of Certified Professional Managers at James Madison University in Harrisonburg, Virginia. He also serves on the Board of Regents for the Institute of Certified Professional Managers.

Gary possesses a number of instructor and consultant certifications. He is one of less than 100 people worldwide that have achieved certification by Inscape Publishing, the original publisher of DiSC® based assessments, as an Inscape Publishing Certified DiSC®

Trainer. He is a contributing author to *180 Ways to Walk the Customer Service Talk*, and has authored numerous articles, including his column *Strategic Trends*™. Gary is currently working on a series of books that combine the wisdom of the American Indian Medicine Wheel with current business research, which includes *Leadership Lessons from the Medicine Wheel*.

Booking Gary Lear

Dynamic, engaging, and thought provoking, Gary is available as a speaker for conference keynotes; company or management retreats; or executive briefing sessions. Don't expect the typical presentation from Gary. His approach is to involve the audience in his sharing of ideas and concepts from the Seven Elements of High Performance™ to bring new insights and understanding to those who are present.

For more information please contact:

Resource Development Systems LLC

934 Falling Creek Dr.
Macon, GA 31220
478-254-3155

Or Visit us on the web at
www.ResourceDevelopmentSystems.com

About Resource Development Systems LLC

Founded in 1997, **Resource Development Systems** LLC is an organizational performance consulting firm dedicated to helping its clients increase performance by being more successful at *Managing the Human Side of Business*sm.

At *RDS* we excel in developing the new critical competencies organizations need to prevail in the global business environment - skills like trust building, collaboration, and innovation. These skills can never be outsourced, replaced, or made obsolete, and they are absolutely key to competing successfully in the world today.

Our development programs are always designed to align people's skills and behavior with organizational strategies to create high performing organizations. That means you have the ability to shape your workforce in alignment with your organization's Vision and its strategies, because our solutions give you a complete system for creating the results you want.

We know change begins with insight, takes shape through action, is intensified by focus, and is fueled by ongoing success.

Insight is Everything – Insight Leads to Engagement – Engagement Leads to Success!

To learn more about our consulting services and programs please contact:

Resource Development Systems LLC

934 Falling Creek Dr.
Macon, GA 31220
478-254-3155

Or Visit us on the web at
www.ResourceDevelopmentSystems.com

The following are the Properties of
Resource Development Systems LLC

The Seven Elements of High Performance™
Managing the Human Side of Business℠
The Four Behaviors that Build Trust™
REAL Goals™
REAL Goal Approach™

The following are the Properties of Inscape Publishing

Adventures in Attitudes®

Some of Our Programs

Team Quest™ Senior Teambuilding Process

Vision Quest™ Strategic Planning Process

Work Engagement Survey™ Organizational Assessment

Leadership Connections™: A Management
Development Process for Engaging Performance

Team DiSCovery™ • Team Innovations™

Accountability in Action™

**Customer Connections™ Sales, Negotiation,
and Customer Service Programs**

All of these programs are based on the Seven Elements
of High Performance™. For more information please
contact **Resource Development Systems** LLC

934 Falling Creek Dr.
Macon, GA 31220
478-254-3155

Or Visit us on the web at

www.ResourceDevelopmentSystems.com

Bibliography and Suggested Readings

The following is a partial list of books that were consulted and/or is suggested for further reading:

A Force for Change: How Leadership Differs from Management, John Kotter, 1990. The Free Press.

A Journey Into the Heroic Environment, Rob Lebow, 1997. Prima Publishing.

A Whole New Mind: Moving from the Information Age to the Conceptual Age, Daniel H. Pink, 2005. Riverhead Books.

Abolishing Performance Appraisals: Why They Backfire and What to do Instead, Tom Coens and Mary Jenkins, 2000. Berrett-Koehler.

Accountability: Freedom and Responsibility without Control, Rob Lebow and Randy Spitzer, 2002. Berrett-Koehler.

Built to Last: Successful Habits of Visionary Companies, James Collins and Jerry Porras, 1997. Harper Business.

Corporate Culture and Performance, John Kotter and James Heskett, 1992. The Free Press.

Death by Meeting, Patrick Lencioni, 2004. Jossey-Bass.

Driving Excellence: How the Aggregate System Turned Microchip Technology from a Failing Company to a Market Leader, Michael J. Jones and Steve Sanghi, 2006. John Wiley & Sons.

Empowerment Takes More Than a Minute: The Essential Keys to Making Empowerment Work in Organizations Large and Small, Ken Blanchard, John P. Carlos and Alan Randolph, 1996. Berrett-Koehler.

Executive Summary: The Integrity Dividend, Tony Simmons, 2000. Cornell University.

First Break All the Rules: What the World's Greatest Managers Do Differently, Marcus Buckingham and Curt Coffman, 1999. The Gallup Organization.

Follow This Path: How the World's Greatest Organizations Drive Growth by Unleashing Human Potential, Curt Coffman and Gabriel Gonzalez-Molina, 2002. The Gallup Organization.

Full Steam Ahead!: Unleash the Power of Vision in Your Company and Your Life, Ken Blanchard and Jesse Stoner, 2003. Berrett-Koehler.

Good to Great: Why Some Companies Make the Leap...and Others Don't, James Collins, 2001. Harper Business.

Gung Ho!: Turn on the People in Any Organization, Ken Blanchard and Sheldon Bowles, 1998. William Marrow and Company.

Hidden Values: How Great Companies Achieve Extraordinary Results with Ordinary People, Charles O'Reilly and Jeffrey Pfeffer, 2000. Harvard Business School Press.

How Full Is your Bucket?: Positive Strategies for Work and Life, Tom Rath and Donald O. Clifton, 2004. Gallup Press.

Innovation on Demand, Allen Fahden, 1993. The Illiterati.

Insights on Leadership: Service, Stewardship, Spirit, and Servant-Leadership, Larry Spears, editor, 1998. John Wiley & Sons.

Intrinsic Motivation at Work: Building Energy and Commitment, Kenneth Thomas, 2002. Berrett-Koehler Publishers.

John P. Kotter on What Leaders Really Do, John Kotter, 1999. Harvard Business Review.

Leadership and the One Minute Manager: Increasing Effectiveness Through Situational Leadership®, Ken Blanchard, Patricia Zigarmi and Drea Zigarmi, 1985. William Marrow and Company.

Managing Transitions: Making the Most of Change 2nd Edition, William Bridges, 2003. Da Capo Press.

Punished by Rewards: The Trouble with Gold Stars, Incentive Plans, A's, Praise, and other Bribes, Alfie Kohn, 1993. Houghton Mifflin.

Raving Fans: A Revolutionary Approach to Customer Service, Ken Blanchard and Sheldon Bowles, 1993. William Marrow and Company.

Rhythms of Learning: Patterns that Bridge Individuals and Organizations, *David Cowan, Journal of Management Inquiry, Sept 95, Vol. 4, Issue 3.*

Servant Leadership: A Journey into the Nature of Legitimate Power & Greatness, Robert Greenleaf, 1977. Paulist Press.

Silos, Politics and Turf Wars, Patrick Lencioni, 2006. Jossey-Bass.

Strategy Maps: Converting Intangible Assets into Tangible Outcomes, Robert S. Kaplan and David P. Norton, 2004. Harvard Business School Publishing.

The Balanced Scorecard: Translating Strategy into Action, Robert S. Kaplan and David P. Norton, 1996. Harvard Business School Publishing.

The Five Dysfunctions of a Team, Patrick Lencioni, 2002. Jossey-Bass.

The Four Obsessions of an Extraordinary Executive, Patrick Lencioni, 2000. Jossey-Bass.

The HR Scorecard: Linking People, Strategy and Performance, Brian E. Bechker, Mark A. Huselid and Dave Ulrich, 2001. Harvard Business School Publishing.

The Human Equation: Building Profits by Putting People First, Jeffrey Pfeffer, 1998. Harvard Business School Publishing.

The Leadership Challenge, James Kouzes and Barry Posner, 2002. Jossey-Bass.

The One-Minute Manager Builds High Performing Teams, Ken Blanchard Donald Carew and Eunice Parisi-Carew, 1990. William Marrow and Company.

The One Thing You Need to Know, Marcus Buckingham, 2005. Free Press.

The Sacred Tree, 1985. *Four Worlds International Institute for Human and Community Development.*

The 7 Hidden Reasons Employees Leave, Leigh Branham, 2005. AMACOM Books.

The Strategy-Focused Organization: How Balanced Scorecard Companies Thrive in the New Business Environment, Robert S. Kaplan and David P. Norton, 2001. Harvard Business School Publishing.

The 3 Keys to Empowerment: Release the Power Within People for Astonishing Results, Ken Blanchard, John P. Carlos and Alan Randolph, 1999. Berrett-Koehler.

The War for Talent, Ed Michaels, Helen Handfield-Jones, and Beth Axelrod, 2001. Harvard Business School Publishing.

Walking on the Wind: Cherokee Teachings for Harmony and Balance, Michael Garrett, 1998. Bear & Company.

Whale Done!: The Power of Positive Relationships, Ken Blanchard, Thad Lacinak, Chuck Thompkins, and Jim Ballard, 2003. The Free Press.

Why Pride Matters More than Money, Jon Katzenbach, 2003. Crown Business.

Why the Bottom Line Isn't: How to Build Value Through People and Organization, Dave Ulrich and Norm Smallwood, 2003. John Wiley & Sons.

Winning, Jack Welch and Suzy Welch, 2005. HarperCollins Publishers.

Wisdom of Teams: Creating the High Performance Organization, Jon Katzenbach and Douglas K. Smith, 2003. Harper Press.

There were numerous research reports and articles also consulted which are not listed here.

TreeNeutral

Printed in the USA
CPSIA information can be obtained
at www.ICGtesting.com
JSHW012034140824
68134JS00033B/3056

9 781599 321110